Word 2002
Simplified®

Save Time!

Download the examples used in this book from our Web site to easily follow along with the steps!

www.maran.com/resources/simplified/word2002

Visual

From
maranGraphics®

&

Hungry Minds™

Best-Selling Books • Digital Downloads • e-books • Answer Networks •
e-Newsletters • Branded Web Sites • e-learning

New York, NY ♦ Cleveland, OH ♦ Indianapolis, IN

D1404737

Word 2002 Simplified®

Published by
Hungry Minds, Inc.
909 Third Avenue
New York, NY 10022
www.hungryminds.com

Copyright© 2002 by maranGraphics Inc.
5755 Coopers Avenue
Mississauga, Ontario, Canada
L4Z 1R9

Library of Congress Control Number: 2001096760
ISBN: 0-7645-3588-9
Printed in the United States of America
10 9 8 7 6 5 4 3 2

1K/QW/QR/QS/MG

Distributed in the United States by Hungry Minds, Inc.
Distributed by CDG Books Canada Inc. for Canada; by Transworld Publishers Limited in the United Kingdom; by IDG Norge Books for Norway; by IDG Sweden Books for Sweden; by IDG Books Australia Publishing Corporation Pty. Ltd. for Australia and New Zealand; by TransQuest Publishers Pte Ltd. for Singapore, Malaysia, Thailand, Indonesia, and Hong Kong; by Gotop Information Inc. for Taiwan; by ICG Muse, Inc. for Japan; by Intersoft for South Africa; by Eyrolles for France; by International Thomson Publishing for Germany, Austria and Switzerland; by Distribuidora Cuspide for Argentina; by LR International for Brazil; by Galileo Libros for Chile; by Ediciones ZETA S.C.R. Ltda. for Peru; by WS Computer Publishing Corporation, Inc. for the Philippines; by Contemporanea de Ediciones for Venezuela; by Express Computer Distributors for the Caribbean and West Indies; by Micronesia Media Distributor, Inc. for Micronesia; by Chips Computadoras S.A. de C.V. for Mexico; by Editorial Norma de Panama S.A. for Panama; by American Bookshops for Finland.
For corporate orders, please call maranGraphics at 800-469-6616 or fax 905-890-9434.
For general information on Hungry Minds' products and services, please contact our Customer Care Department within the U.S. at 800-762-2974, outside the U.S. at 317-572-3993 or fax 317-572-4002.
For sales inquiries and reseller information, including discounts, premium and bulk quantity sales, and foreign-language translations, please contact our Customer Care Department at 800-434-3422, fax 317-572-4002, or write to Hungry Minds, Inc., Attn: Customer Care Department, 10475 Crosspoint Boulevard, Indianapolis, IN 46256.
For information on licensing foreign or domestic rights, please contact our Sub-Rights Customer Care Department at 212-844-5000.
For information on using Hungry Minds' products and services in the classroom or for ordering examination copies, please contact our Educational Sales Department at 800-434-2086 or fax 317-572-4005.
For press review copies, author interviews, or other publicity information, please contact our Public Relations department at 317-572-3168 or fax 317-572-4168.
For authorization to photocopy items for corporate, personal, or educational use, please contact maranGraphics at the address above.

Trademark Acknowledgments

Permissions

is a trademark of
Hungry Minds™ Hungry Minds, Inc.

U.S. Corporate Sales	**U.S. Trade Sales**
Contact maranGraphics at (800) 469-6616 or fax (905) 890-9434.	Contact Hungry Minds at (800) 434-3422 or fax (317) 572-4002.

Some comments from our readers...

"Compliments To The Chef!! Your books are extraordinary! Or, simply put, Extra-Ordinary, meaning way above the rest! THANK YOU THANK YOU THANK YOU! for creating these. I buy them for friends, family, and colleagues."
— *Christine J. Manfrin (Castle Rock, CO)*

"What fantastic teaching books you have produced! Congratulations to you and your staff. You deserve the Nobel prize in Education in the Software category. Thanks for helping me to understand computers."
— *Bruno Tonon (Melbourne, Australia)*

"I was introduced to maranGraphics about four years ago and YOU ARE THE GREATEST THING THAT EVER HAPPENED TO INTRODUCTORY COMPUTER BOOKS!"
— *Glenn Nettleton (Huntsville, AL)*

"I'm a grandma who was pushed by an 11-year-old grandson to join the computer age. I found myself hopelessly confused and frustrated until I discovered the Visual series. I'm no expert by any means now, but I'm a lot further along than I would have been otherwise. Thank you!"
— *Carol Louthain (Logansport, IN)*

"Thank you, thank you, thank you...for making it so easy for me to break into this high-tech world. I now own four of your books. I recommend them to anyone who is a beginner like myself. Now...if you could just do one for programming VCRs, it would make my day!"
— *Gay O'Donnell (Calgary, Alberta, Canada)*

"I write to extend my thanks and appreciation for your books. They are clear, easy to follow, and straight to the point. Keep up the good work!"
— *Seward Kollie (Dakar, Senegal)*

"Thank you for making it a lot easier to learn the basics."
— *Allan Black (Woodlawn, Ontario, Canada)*

"Your books are superior! An avid reader since childhood, I've consumed literally tens of thousands of books, a significant quantity in the learning/teaching category. Your series is the most precise, visually appealing, and compelling to peruse. Kudos!"
— *Margaret Chmilar (Edmonton, Alberta, Canada)*

"I just want to tell you how much I, a true beginner, really enjoy your books and now understand a lot more about my computer and working with Windows. I'm 51 and a long time out of the classroom, but these books make it easier for me to learn. Hats off to you for a great product."
— *William K. Rodgers (Spencer, NC)*

"I would like to take this time to thank you and your company for producing great and easy to learn products. I bought two of your books from a local bookstore, and it was the best investment I've ever made!"
— *Jeff Eastman (West Des Moines, IA)*

"I would like to take this time to compliment maranGraphics on creating such great books. Thank you for making it clear. Keep up the good work."
— *Kirk Santoro (Burbank, CA)*

"I have to praise you and your company on the fine products you turn out. Thank you for creating books that are easy to follow. Keep turning out those quality books."
— *Gordon Justin (Brielle, NJ)*

"Over time, I have bought a number of your 'Read Less-Learn More' books. For me, they are THE way to learn anything easily. I learn easiest using your method of teaching."
— *José A. Mazón (Cuba, NY)*

maranGraphics is a family-run business located near Toronto, Canada.

At **maranGraphics**, we believe in producing great computer books—one book at a time.

Each maranGraphics book uses the award-winning communication process that we have been developing over the last 25 years. Using this process, we organize screen shots, text and illustrations in a way that makes it easy for you to learn new concepts and tasks.

We spend hours deciding the best way to perform each task, so you don't have to! Our clear, easy-to-follow screen shots and instructions walk you through each task from beginning to end.

Our detailed illustrations go hand-in-hand with the text to help reinforce the information. Each illustration is a labor of love—some take up to a week to draw!

We want to thank you for purchasing what we feel are the best computer books money can buy. We hope you enjoy using this book as much as we enjoyed creating it!

Sincerely,

The Maran Family

Please visit us on the Web at:
www.maran.com

Credits

Author:
Ruth Maran

Copy Development Director:
Wanda Lawrie

Copy Editing and Screen Captures:
Roxanne Van Damme
Megan Kirby

Technical Consultant:
Paul Whitehead

Project Manager:
Judy Maran

Editor:
Norm Schumacher

Layout Artist:
Treena Lees

Illustrators:
Russ Marini
Steven Schaerer

Screen Artist and Illustrator:
Darryl Grossi

Indexer:
Roxanne Van Damme

Permissions Coordinator:
Jennifer Amaral

Senior Vice President and Publisher, Hungry Minds Technology Publishing Group:
Richard Swadley

Publishing Director, Hungry Minds Technology Publishing Group:
Barry Pruett

Editorial Support, Hungry Minds Technology Publishing Group:
Jennifer Dorsey
Sandy Rodrigues
Lindsay Sandman

Post Production:
Robert Maran

Acknowledgments

Thanks to the dedicated staff of maranGraphics, including
Jennifer Amaral, Roderick Anatalio, Darryl Grossi,
Kelleigh Johnson, Megan Kirby, Wanda Lawrie,
Treena Lees, Cathy Lo, Jill Maran, Judy Maran,
Robert Maran, Ruth Maran, Russ Marini, Steven Schaerer,
Norm Schumacher, Raquel Scott, Roxanne Van Damme
and Paul Whitehead.

Finally, to Richard Maran who originated the easy-to-use
graphic format of this guide. Thank you for your
inspiration and guidance.

Table of Contents

CHAPTER

EDIT TEXT

CHAPTER

FORMAT TEXT

Table of Contents

CHAPTER 6

FORMAT PAGES

CHAPTER 7

PRINT DOCUMENTS

CHAPTER 8

WORK WITH TABLES

WORD

The New Orleans Blues

Scene i)

Tim and Jeff are sitting on the front steps of their house on a side street in New Orleans. Tim is trying to convince his son to let go of his dream of becoming a famous jazz saxophonist. Upset with his father for meddling in his life, Jeff storms off down the street.

Scene ii)

Tim goes inside the house to join Kathleen in the kitchen. As Kathleen **prepares** dinner, they discuss their son's future. Jacqueline, their guest, arrives and they all reminisce about their youth.

Scene iii)

Later in the evening, Jeff and Constance arrive at the house. Jeff his saxophone out of his case and begins playing a quiet as Constan ins his to Constan

prepares

CHAPTER 1

GETTING STARTED

Are you ready to begin using Microsoft Word 2002? This chapter will help you get started.

INTRODUCTION TO WORD

Word is a word processing program you can use to efficiently produce professional-looking documents, such as letters, reports, essays and newsletters.

Edit Documents

Word offers many time-saving features to help you edit text in a document. You can add, delete and rearrange text. You can also quickly count the number of words in a document, check your document for spelling and grammar errors and use Word's thesaurus to find more suitable words.

Format Documents

You can format a document to enhance the appearance of the document. You can use various fonts, styles and colors to emphasize important text. You can also adjust the spacing between lines of text, change the margins, center text on a page and create newspaper columns.

Print Documents

You can produce a paper copy of a document you create. Before printing, you can preview how the document will appear on a printed page. Word also allows you to print envelopes and labels.

Work With Tables and Graphics

Word can help you create tables to neatly display columns of information in a document. Word's ready-to-use designs allow you to instantly give a table a professional appearance. You can also add graphics, such as AutoShapes, clip art images and diagrams, to a document to illustrate ideas.

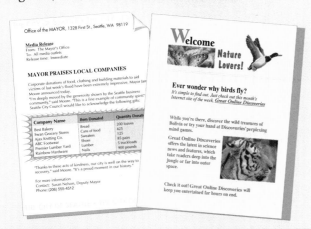

Use Mail Merge

Word's Mail Merge Wizard can help you quickly produce personalized letters and labels for each person on a mailing list. This is useful if you often send the same document, such as an announcement or advertisement, to many people.

Use Speech Recognition

The speech recognition feature allows you to use your voice to enter text into a document. You can also use speech recognition to select commands from menus, toolbars and dialog boxes using your voice.

Word and the Internet

Word offers features that allow you to take advantage of the Internet. You can create a hyperlink in a document to connect the document to a Web page. You can also save a document as a Web page. This allows you to place the document on the Internet for other people to view.

You can start Word to create and work with documents.

When you start Word, a blank document appears on your screen. You can type text into this document.

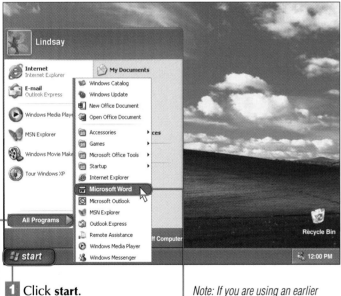

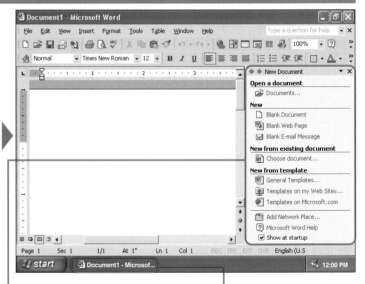

1 Click **start**.

2 Click **All Programs** to view a list of the programs on your computer.

Note: If you are using an earlier version of Windows, click ***Programs*** *in step* ***2***.

3 Click **Microsoft Word**.

■ The Microsoft Word window appears, displaying a blank document.

■ This area displays a task pane, which allows you to quickly perform common tasks. For information on using the task pane, see page 16.

■ A button for the Microsoft Word window appears on the taskbar.

The Word window displays many items you can use to create and work with your documents.

Title Bar

Shows the name of the displayed document.

Menu Bar

Provides access to lists of commands available in Word and displays an area where you can type a question to get help information.

Standard Toolbar

Contains buttons you can use to select common commands, such as Save and Print.

Formatting Toolbar

Contains buttons you can use to select common formatting commands, such as Bold and Italic.

Ruler

Allows you to change tab and indent settings for your documents.

Task Pane

Contains options you can select to perform common tasks, such as opening or creating a document.

Insertion Point

The flashing line on the screen that indicates where the text you type will appear.

Document Views

Provides access to four different views of your documents.

Scroll Bars

Allow you to browse through a document.

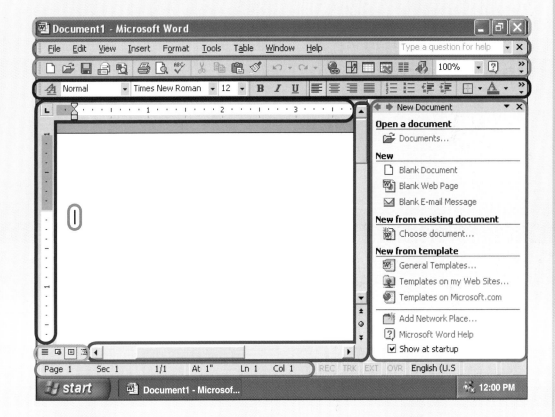

Status Bar

Provides information about the area of the document displayed on the screen and the position of the insertion point.

Page 1

The page displayed on the screen.

Sec 1

The section of the document displayed on the screen.

1/1

The page displayed on the screen and the total number of pages in the document.

At 1"

The distance from the top of the page to the insertion point.

Ln 1

The number of lines from the top margin to the insertion point.

Col 1

The number of characters from the left margin to the insertion point, including spaces.

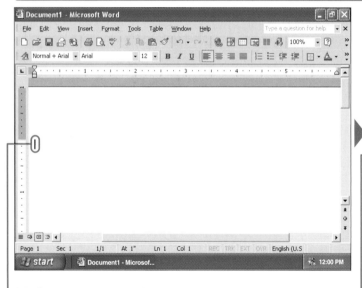

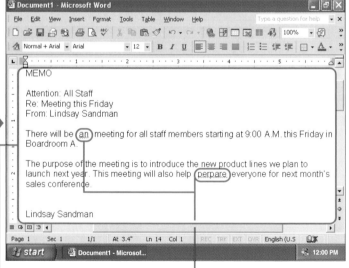

■ The text you type will appear where the insertion point flashes on your screen.

1 Type the text for your document.

Note: In this book, the font of text was changed to Arial to make the examples easier to read. To change the font of text, see page 78.

■ When you reach the end of a line, Word automatically wraps the text to the next line. You only need to press the **Enter** key when you want to start a new paragraph.

■ Word automatically underlines misspelled words in red and grammar errors in green. The underlines will not appear when you print your document. To correct misspelled words and grammar errors, see page 58.

How can I quickly enter text in a new location in my document?

Word's Click and Type feature allows you to quickly position the insertion point in a new location so you can enter text. Double-click a blank area where you want to position the insertion point and then type the text you want to enter. The Click and Type feature is only available in the Print Layout and Web Layout views. To change the view of a document, see page 36.

Where can I find a sample document like the one used in this chapter?

The sample documents used in each chapter of this book are available on the Web at www.maran.com/resources/teachyourself/ word2002. You can download the sample documents so you can perform the tasks in this book without having to type the documents yourself.

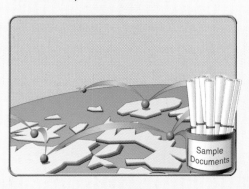

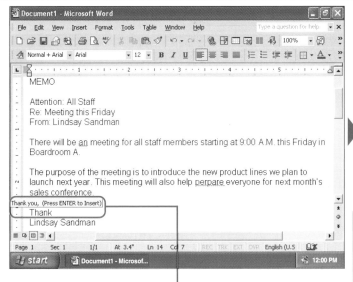

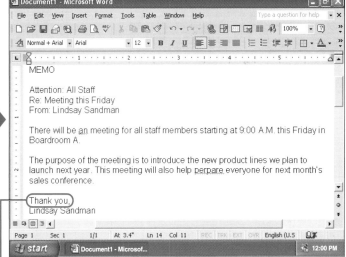

ENTER TEXT AUTOMATICALLY

■ Word's AutoText feature helps you quickly enter common words and phrases.

■ When you type the first few characters of a common word or phrase, a yellow box appears, displaying the text.

1 To insert the text, press the `Enter` key.

■ To ignore the text, continue typing.

Note: For more information on the AutoText feature, see page 64.

Before performing many tasks in Word, you must select the text you want to work with. Selected text appears highlighted on your screen.

SELECT TEXT

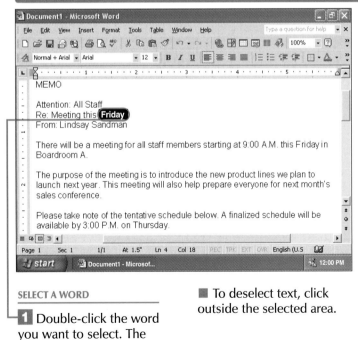

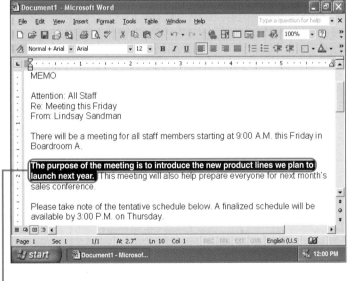

SELECT A WORD

1 Double-click the word you want to select. The word is highlighted.

■ To deselect text, click outside the selected area.

SELECT A SENTENCE

1 Press and hold down the **Ctrl** key as you click the sentence you want to select.

10

How do I select a paragraph or a large area of text?

To select a paragraph, position the mouse I over the paragraph you want to select and then quickly click **three** times.

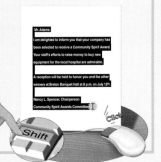

To select a large area of text, click at the beginning of the text. Then press and hold down the **Shift** key as you click at the end of the text.

Can I select multiple areas of text in my document?

Yes. To select multiple areas of text, press and hold down the **Ctrl** key as you select each area.

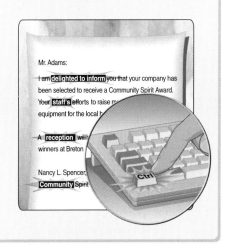

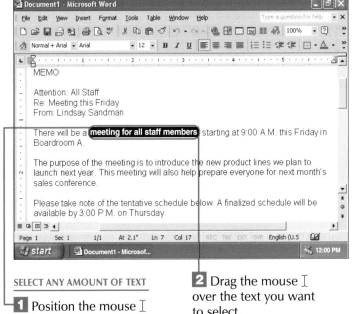

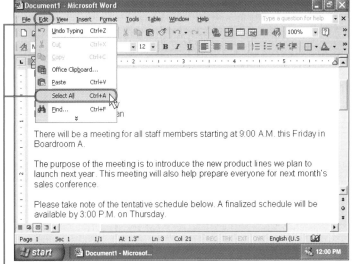

SELECT ANY AMOUNT OF TEXT

1 Position the mouse I over the first word you want to select.

2 Drag the mouse I over the text you want to select.

SELECT ENTIRE DOCUMENT

1 Click **Edit**.

2 Click **Select All** to select all the text in your document.

Note: You can also press and hold down the **Ctrl** *key as you press the* **A** *key to select all the text in your document.*

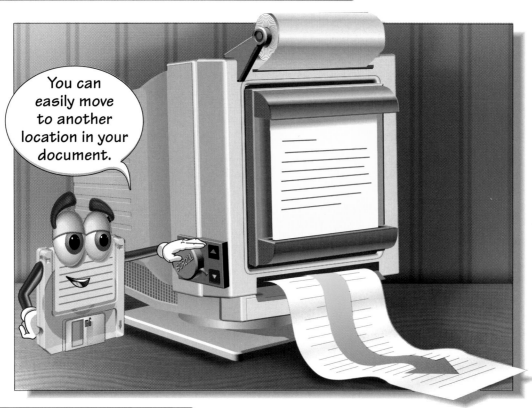

If your document contains a lot of text, your computer screen may not be able to display all the text at once. You must scroll through your document to view other parts of the document.

MOVE THROUGH A DOCUMENT

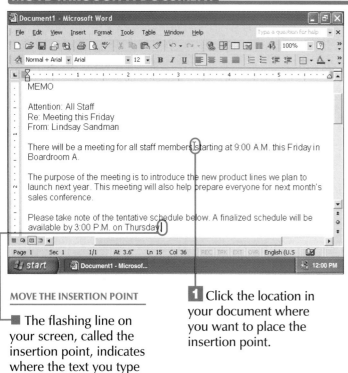

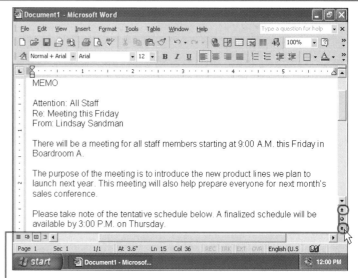

MOVE THE INSERTION POINT

■ The flashing line on your screen, called the insertion point, indicates where the text you type will appear.

1 Click the location in your document where you want to place the insertion point.

DISPLAY PREVIOUS OR NEXT PAGE

1 To display the previous or next page, click one of the following buttons.

± Display previous page

∓ Display next page

How can I use my keyboard to move through a document?

You can press the ←, →, ↑ or ↓ key to move through a document one character or line at a time. You can press the Page Up or Page Down key to move through a document one screen at a time.

How do I use the wheel on my mouse to scroll through a document?

You can purchase a mouse with a wheel between the left and right mouse buttons. Moving this wheel allows you to quickly scroll through a document.

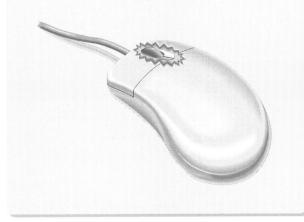

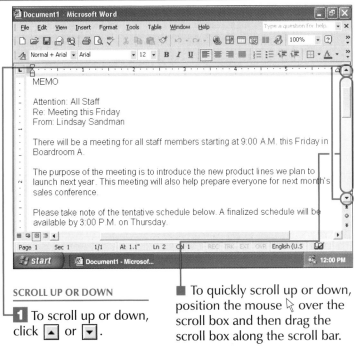

SCROLL UP OR DOWN

1 To scroll up or down, click ▲ or ▼.

■ To quickly scroll up or down, position the mouse ⌖ over the scroll box and then drag the scroll box along the scroll bar.

Note: The location of the scroll box indicates which part of the document you are viewing. To view the middle of the document, drag the scroll box halfway down the scroll bar.

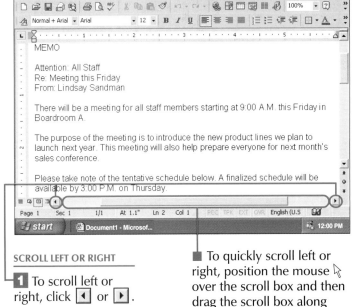

SCROLL LEFT OR RIGHT

1 To scroll left or right, click ◄ or ►.

■ To quickly scroll left or right, position the mouse ⌖ over the scroll box and then drag the scroll box along the scroll bar.

You can select a command from a menu or toolbar to perform a task in Word.

When you first start Word, the most commonly used commands and buttons appear on each menu and toolbar. As you work, Word customizes the menus and toolbars to display the commands and buttons you use most often.

SELECT A COMMAND

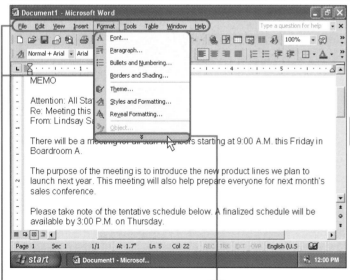

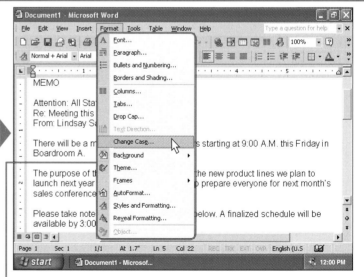

USING MENUS

1 Click the name of the menu you want to display.

■ A short version of the menu appears, displaying the most commonly used commands.

2 To expand the menu and display all the commands, position the mouse ⍉ over ⯆.

Note: If you do not perform step 2, the expanded menu will automatically appear after a few seconds.

■ The expanded menu appears, displaying all the commands.

3 Click the command you want to use.

Note: A dimmed command is currently not available.

■ To close a menu without selecting a command, click outside the menu.

How can I make a command appear on the short version of a menu?

When you select a command from an expanded menu, the command is automatically added to the short version of the menu. The next time you display the short version of the menu, the command you selected will appear.

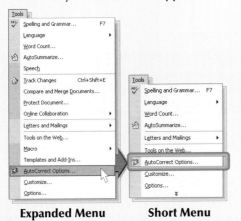

Expanded Menu   **Short Menu**

How can I quickly select a command?

You can use a shortcut menu to quickly select a command.

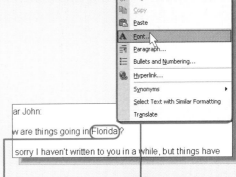

1 Right-click an item to display a shortcut menu. The shortcut menu displays the most frequently used commands for the item.

2 Click the command you want to use.

■ To close a shortcut menu without selecting a command, click outside the menu.

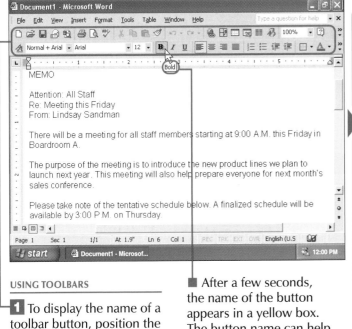

USING TOOLBARS

1 To display the name of a toolbar button, position the mouse over the button.

■ After a few seconds, the name of the button appears in a yellow box. The button name can help you determine the task the button performs.

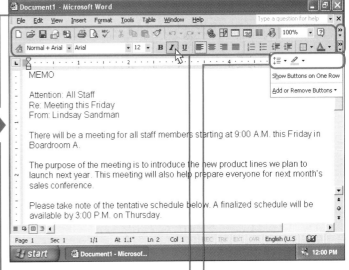

2 A toolbar may not be able to display all of its buttons. Click to display additional buttons for the toolbar.

■ Additional buttons for the toolbar appear.

3 To use a toolbar button to select a command, click the button.

USING THE TASK PANE

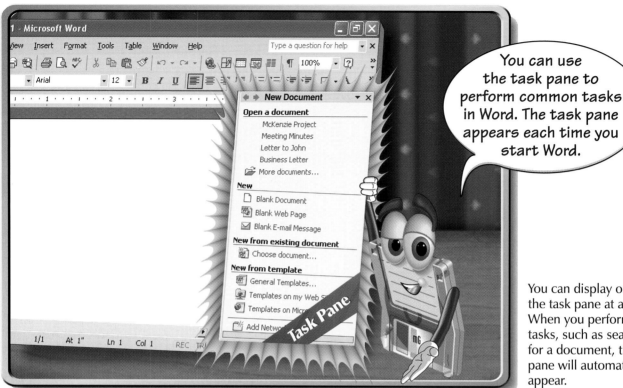

> You can use the task pane to perform common tasks in Word. The task pane appears each time you start Word.

You can display or hide the task pane at any time. When you perform some tasks, such as searching for a document, the task pane will automatically appear.

USING THE TASK PANE

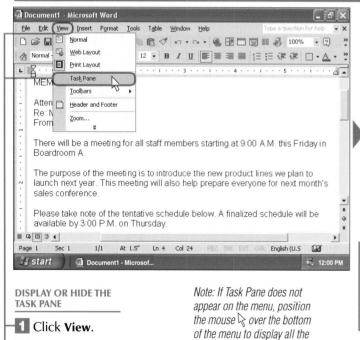

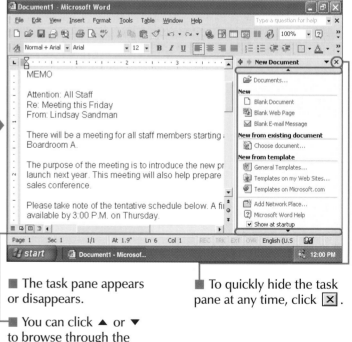

DISPLAY OR HIDE THE TASK PANE

1 Click **View**.

2 Click **Task Pane**.

Note: If Task Pane does not appear on the menu, position the mouse ⬉ over the bottom of the menu to display all the menu options.

■ The task pane appears or disappears.

■ You can click ▲ or ▼ to browse through the information in the task pane.

■ To quickly hide the task pane at any time, click ✖.

What are some of the task panes available in Word?

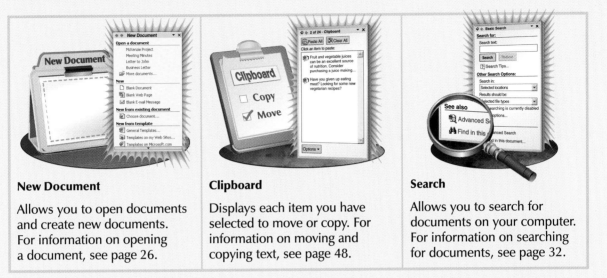

New Document

Allows you to open documents and create new documents. For information on opening a document, see page 26.

Clipboard

Displays each item you have selected to move or copy. For information on moving and copying text, see page 48.

Search

Allows you to search for documents on your computer. For information on searching for documents, see page 32.

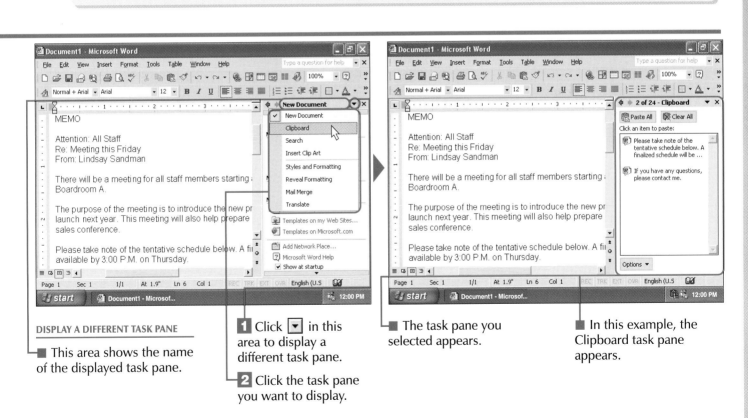

DISPLAY A DIFFERENT TASK PANE

■ This area shows the name of the displayed task pane.

1 Click ▾ in this area to display a different task pane.

2 Click the task pane you want to display.

■ The task pane you selected appears.

■ In this example, the Clipboard task pane appears.

> If you do not know how to perform a task in Word, you can ask a question to find help information for the task. Asking a question allows you to quickly find help information of interest.

GETTING HELP

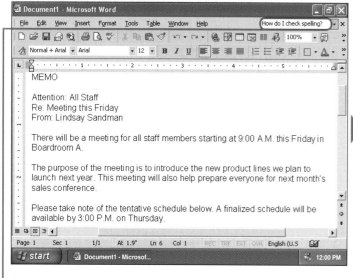

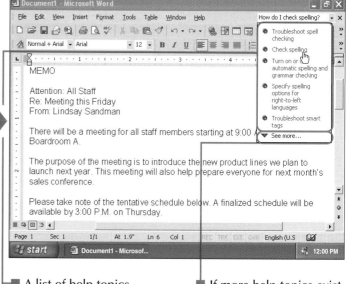

1 Click this area and type your question. Then press the **Enter** key.

■ A list of help topics related to your question appears.

2 Click a help topic of interest.

■ If more help topics exist, you can click **See more** to view the additional topics.

What other ways can I obtain help?

In the Microsoft Word Help window, you can use the following tabs to obtain help information.

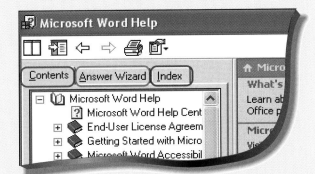

Index

You can double-click a word in the alphabetical list of keywords to display help topics related to the word.

Contents

You can double-click a book icon (📖) or click a page icon (❓) to browse through the contents of Microsoft Word Help.

Answer Wizard

You can type a question and then press the `Enter` key to display help topics related to the question.

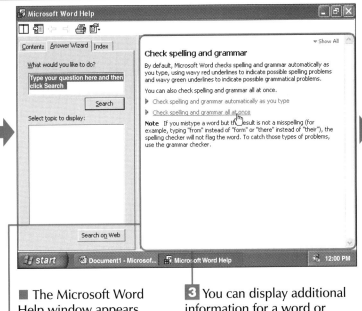

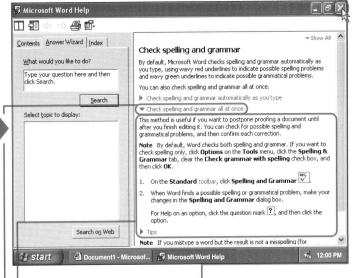

■ The Microsoft Word Help window appears.

Note: To maximize the Microsoft Word Help window to fill your screen, click 🔲 in the top right corner of the window.

■ This area displays information about the help topic you selected.

3 You can display additional information for a word or phrase that appears in color. To display the additional information for a colored word or phrase, click the word or phrase.

■ The additional information appears.

Note: The additional information may be a definition, series of steps or tips.

■ To once again hide the additional information, click the colored word or phrase.

4 When you finish reviewing the help information, click ✖ to close the Microsoft Word Help window.

CHAPTER 2

SAVE AND OPEN DOCUMENTS

Are you wondering how to save, close or open a Word document? Learn how in this chapter.

SAVE A DOCUMENT

You can save your document to store it for future use. Saving a document allows you to later review and edit the document.

SAVE A DOCUMENT

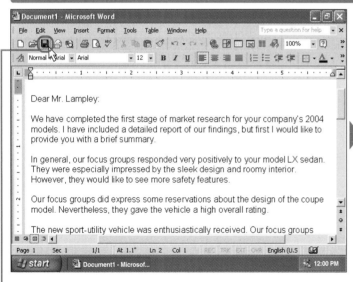

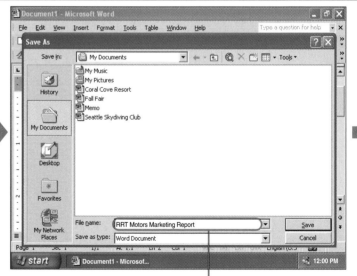

1 Click 🖬 to save your document.

Note: If 🖬 is not displayed, click ⋙ on the Standard toolbar to display the button.

■ The Save As dialog box appears.

Note: If you previously saved your document, the Save As dialog box will not appear since you have already named the document.

2 Type a name for the document.

Note: A document name cannot contain the * : ? > < | or " characters.

What are the commonly used locations that I can access?

History

Provides access to folders and documents you recently worked with.

My Documents

Provides a convenient place to store a document.

Desktop

Allows you to store a document on the Windows desktop.

Favorites

Provides a place to store a document you will frequently use.

My Network Places

Allows you to store a document on your network.

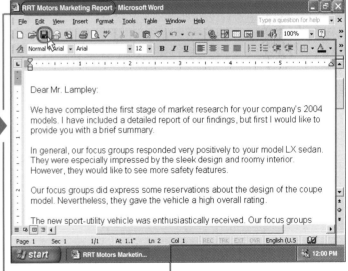

■ This area shows the location where Word will store your document. You can click this area to change the location.

■ This area allows you to access commonly used locations. You can click a location to save your document in the location.

3 Click **Save** to save your document.

■ Word saves your document and displays the name of the document at the top of your screen.

SAVE CHANGES

You should regularly save changes you make to a document to avoid losing your work.

1 Click 🖫 to save the changes you made to your document.

23

When you finish working with a document, you can close the document to remove it from your screen.

When you close a document, you do not exit the Word program. You can continue to work with other documents.

CLOSE A DOCUMENT

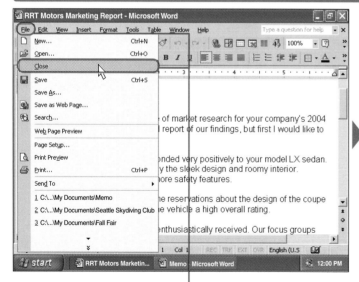

■ Before closing a document, you should save any changes you made to the document. To save a document, see page 22.

▬1 Click **File**.

▬2 Click **Close** to close the document.

■ The document disappears from your screen.

■ If you had more than one document open, the second last document you worked with appears on your screen.

When you finish using Word, you can exit the program.

You should always exit all open programs before turning off your computer.

EXIT WORD

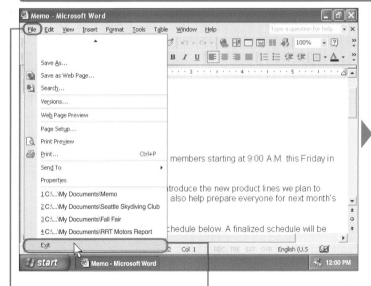

■ Before exiting Word, you should save all your open documents. To save a document, see page 22.

1 Click **File**.

2 Click **Exit**.

Note: If Exit does not appear on the menu, position the mouse over the bottom of the menu to display all the menu options.

■ The Microsoft Word window disappears from your screen.

■ The button for the Microsoft Word window disappears from the taskbar.

OPEN A DOCUMENT

You can open a saved document to view the document on your screen. Opening a document allows you to review and make changes to the document.

OPEN A DOCUMENT

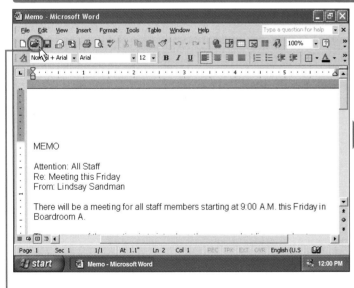

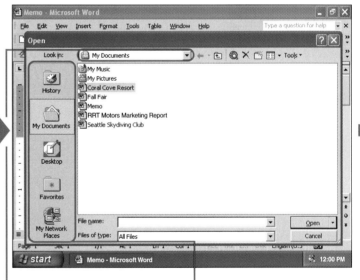

1 Click 📂 to open a document.

Note: If 📂 is not displayed, click ⋮ on the Standard toolbar to display the button.

■ The Open dialog box appears.

■ This area shows the location of the displayed documents. You can click this area to change the location.

■ This area allows you to access documents stored in commonly used locations. You can click a location to display the documents stored in the location.

Note: For information on the commonly used locations, see the top of page 23.

SIMPLIFY IT

How can I quickly open a document I recently worked with?

Word remembers the names of the last four documents you worked with. You can use one of the following methods to quickly open one of these documents.

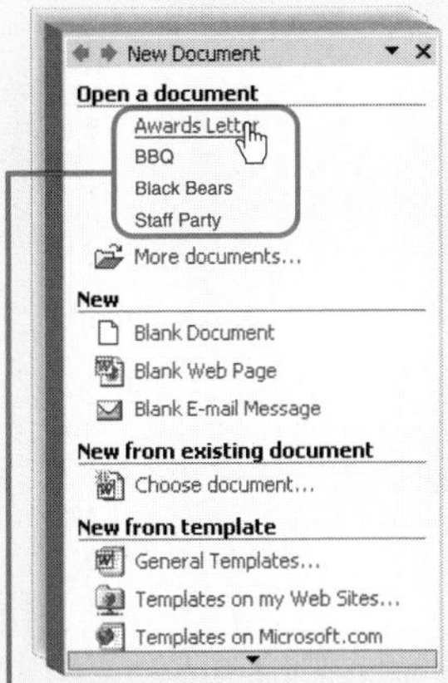

Use the Task Pane

The New Document task pane appears each time you start Word. To display the New Document task pane, see page 16.

1 Click the name of the document you want to open.

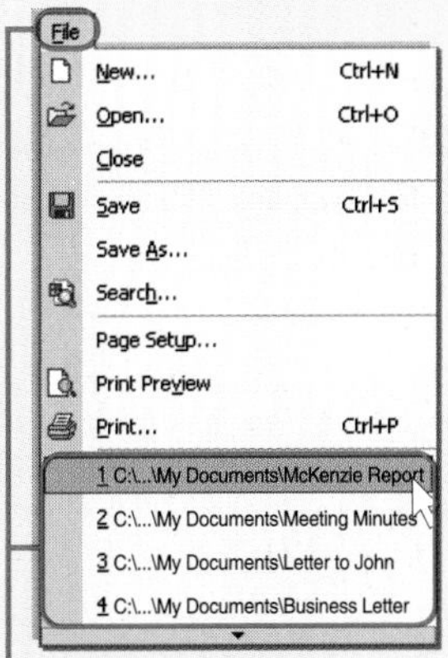

Use the File Menu

1 Click **File**.

2 Click the name of the document you want to open.

Note: If the names of the last four documents you worked with are not all displayed, position the mouse over the bottom of the menu to display all the names.

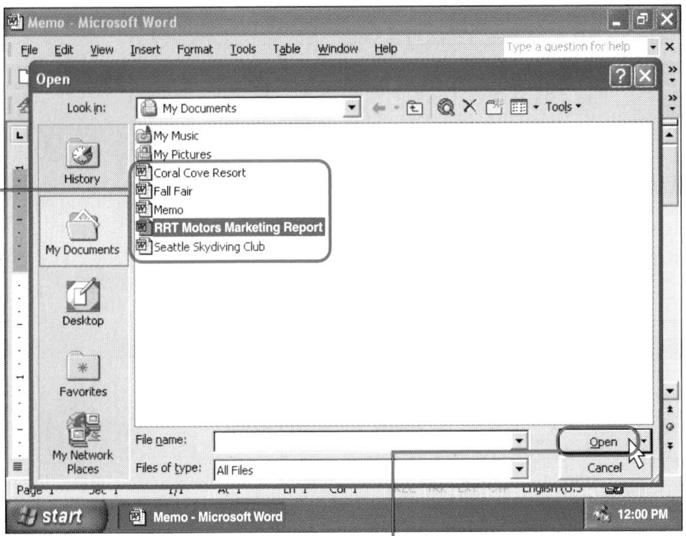

2 Click the name of the document you want to open.

3 Click **Open** to open the document.

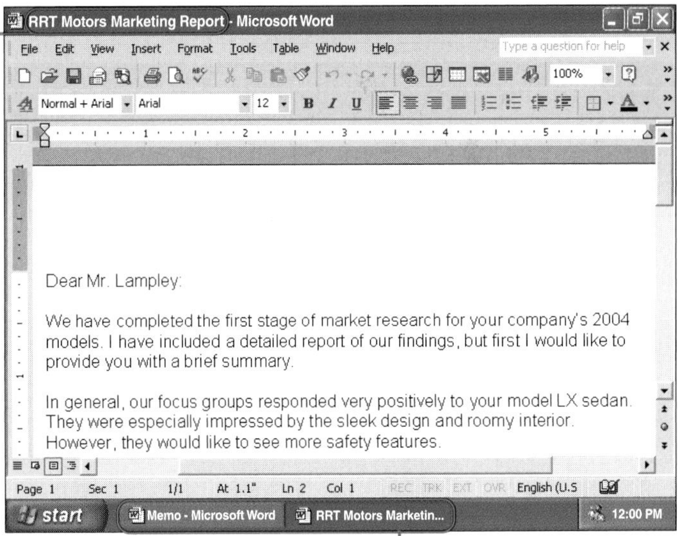

■ The document opens and appears on your screen. You can now review and make changes to the document.

■ This area displays the name of the document.

■ If you already had a document open, the new document appears in a new Microsoft Word window. You can click the buttons on the taskbar to switch between the open documents.

CREATE A NEW DOCUMENT

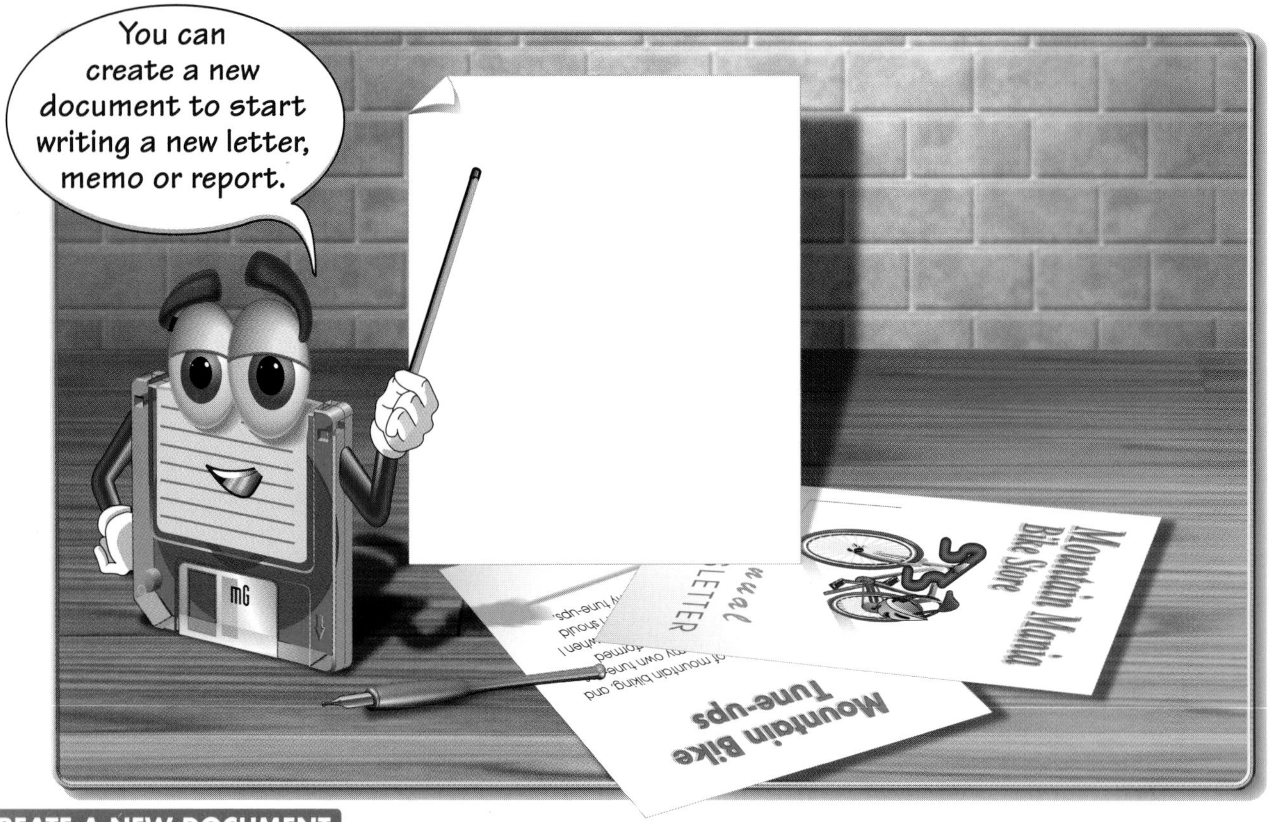
You can create a new document to start writing a new letter, memo or report.
Mountain Mania Bike Store
Mountain Bike Tune-ups

CREATE A NEW DOCUMENT

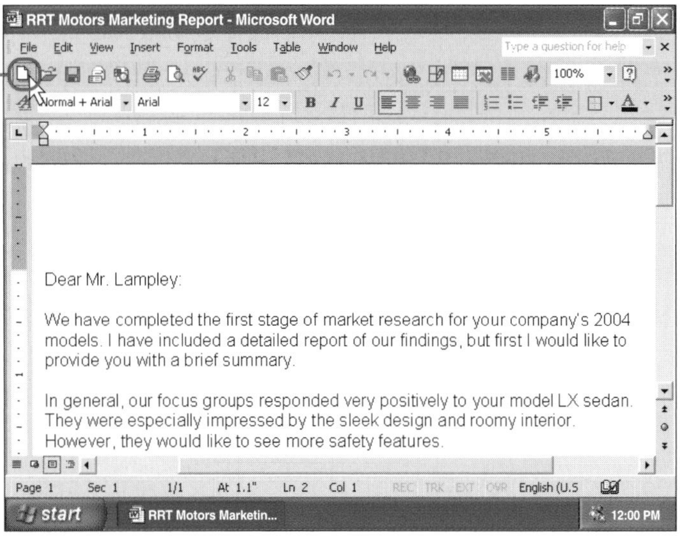
RRT Motors Marketing Report - Microsoft Word
Dear Mr. Lampley:
We have completed the first stage of market research for your company's 2004 models. I have included a detailed report of our findings, but first I would like to provide you with a brief summary.
In general, our focus groups responded very positively to your model LX sedan. They were especially impressed by the sleek design and roomy interior. However, they would like to see more safety features.
start
RRT Motors Marketin...
12:00 PM

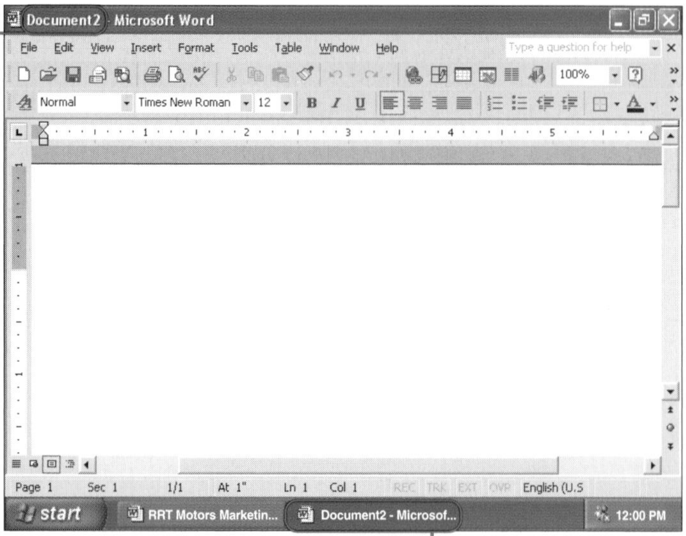
Document2 - Microsoft Word
start
RRT Motors Marketin...
Document2 - Microsof...
12:00 PM

1 Click to create a new document.

Note: If is not displayed, click on the Standard toolbar to display the button.

■ A new document appears. The previous document is now hidden behind the new document.

■ Word gives the new document a temporary name, such as Document2, until you save the document. To save a document, see page 22.

■ A button for the new document appears on the taskbar.

You can have several documents open at once. Word allows you to easily switch from one open document to another.

SWITCH BETWEEN DOCUMENTS

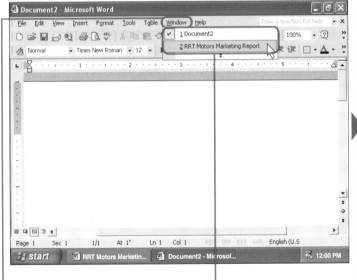

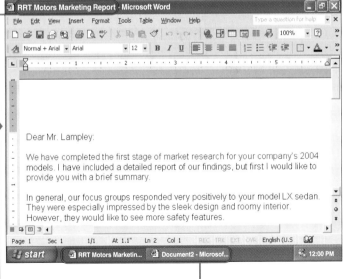

1 Click **Window** to display a list of all the documents you have open.

2 Click the name of the document you want to switch to.

■ The document appears.

■ This area shows the name of the displayed document.

■ The taskbar displays a button for each open document. You can also click the buttons on the taskbar to switch between the open documents.

USING TEMPLATES AND WIZARDS

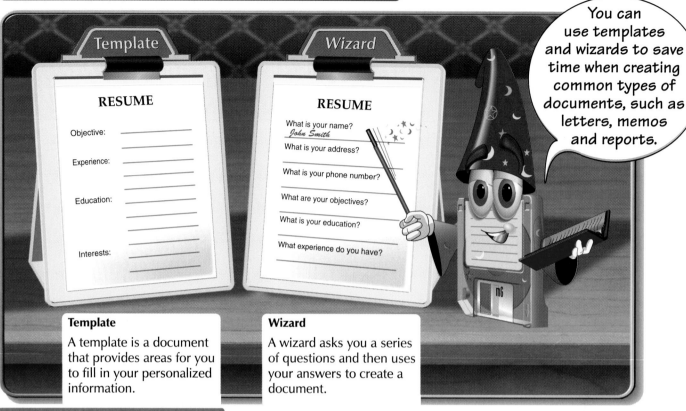

You can use templates and wizards to save time when creating common types of documents, such as letters, memos and reports.

Template

A template is a document that provides areas for you to fill in your personalized information.

Wizard

A wizard asks you a series of questions and then uses your answers to create a document.

USING TEMPLATES AND WIZARDS

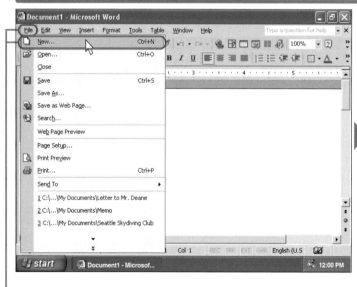

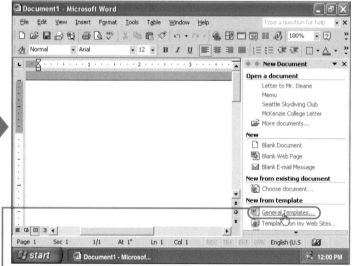

1 Click **File**.

2 Click **New**.

■ The New Document task pane appears.

3 Click **General Templates**.

*Note: If you cannot see the **General Templates** option, click ▼ to scroll down through the New Document task pane.*

■ The Templates dialog box appears.

Why does a dialog box appear when I select a template or wizard?

A dialog box appears if the template or wizard you selected is not installed on your computer. Insert the CD-ROM disc you used to install Word into your computer's CD-ROM drive. Then click **OK** to install the template or wizard.

How can I quickly begin using a template or wizard I recently worked with?

The New Document task pane displays the names of the last two templates or wizards you worked with. To display the New Document task pane, perform steps **1** and **2** on page 30.

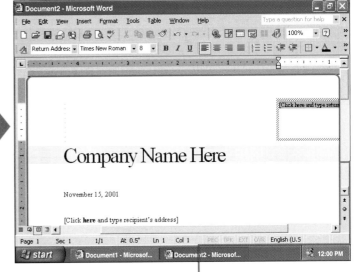

1 To quickly begin using a template or wizard, click the name of the template or wizard you want to use.

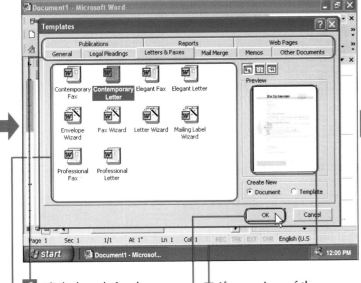

4 Click the tab for the type of document you want to create.

5 Click the template or wizard for the document you want to create.

Note: The icon for a wizard displays a magic wand (✦).

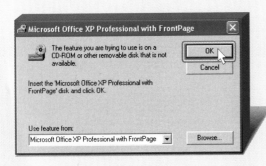

■ If a preview of the document you selected is available, the preview appears in this area.

6 Click **OK** to create the document.

■ The document appears on your screen.

Note: If you selected a wizard in step 5, Word will ask you a series of questions before creating the document.

7 Type your personalized information in the appropriate areas to complete the document.

SEARCH FOR A DOCUMENT

If you cannot remember the name or location of a document you want to work with, you can search for the document.

SEARCH FOR A DOCUMENT

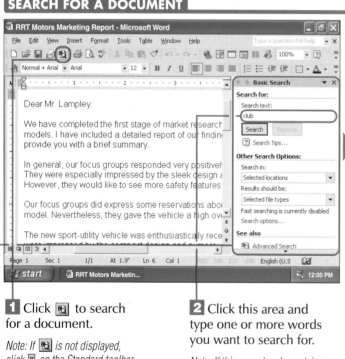

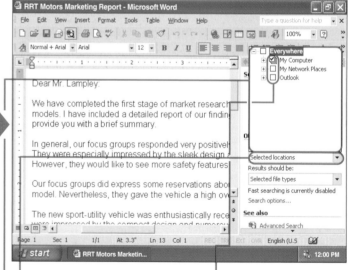

1 Click 🔍 to search for a document.

Note: If 🔍 is not displayed, click ⏷ on the Standard toolbar to display the button.

■ The Search task pane appears.

2 Click this area and type one or more words you want to search for.

Note: If this area already contains text, drag the mouse I over the existing text and then press the Delete key. Then perform step 2.

3 Click ⏷ in this area to select the locations you want to search.

■ A check mark (✔) appears beside each location Word will search.

Note: By default, Word will search all the drives and folders on your computer.

4 You can click the box beside a location to add (✔) or remove (☐) a check mark.

5 To close the list of locations, click outside the list.

How will Word use the words I specify to search for documents?

Word will search the contents of documents and the file names of documents for the words you specify. When searching the contents of documents, Word will search for various forms of the words. For example, searching for "run" will find "run," "running" and "ran."

When selecting the locations and types of files I want to search for, how can I display more items?

Each item that displays a plus sign (⊞) contains hidden items. To display the hidden items, click the plus sign (⊞) beside the item (⊞ changes to ⊟). To once again hide the items, click the minus sign (⊟) beside the item.

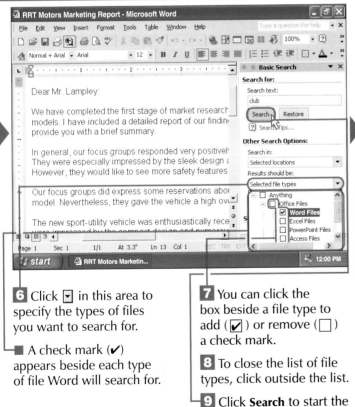

6 Click ▾ in this area to specify the types of files you want to search for.

■ A check mark (✔) appears beside each type of file Word will search for.

7 You can click the box beside a file type to add (✔) or remove (☐) a check mark.

8 To close the list of file types, click outside the list.

9 Click **Search** to start the search.

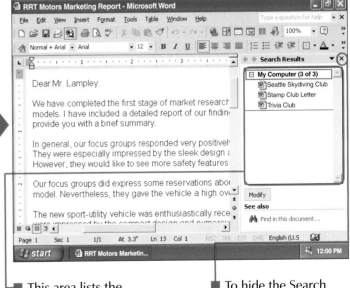

■ This area lists the documents that contain the words you specified.

■ To open a document in the list, click the document.

■ To hide the Search task pane at any time, click ☒.

CHAPTER 3

CHANGE DISPLAY OF DOCUMENTS

Are you interested in changing the way your document appears on your screen? In this chapter, you will learn how to display your document in a different view, display or hide a toolbar and more.

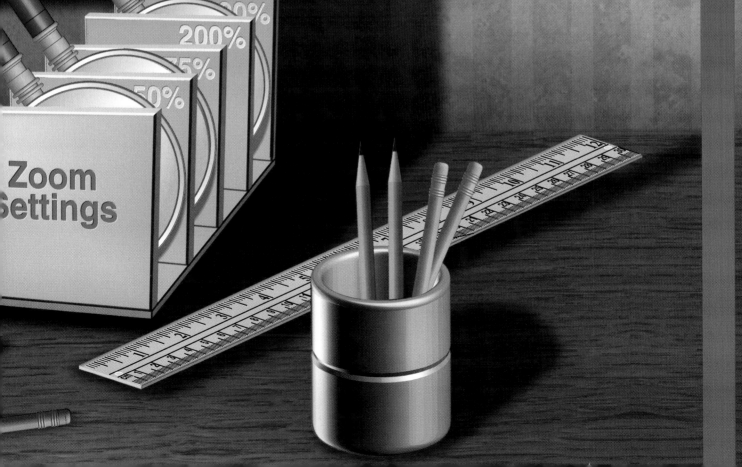

CHANGE THE VIEW OF A DOCUMENT

Word offers four different views that you can use to display your document. You can choose the view that best suits your needs.

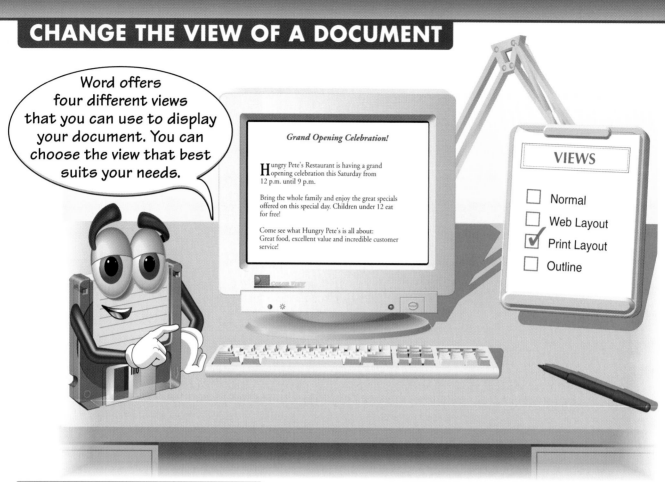

VIEWS

- ☐ Normal
- ☐ Web Layout
- ☑ Print Layout
- ☐ Outline

CHANGE THE VIEW OF A DOCUMENT

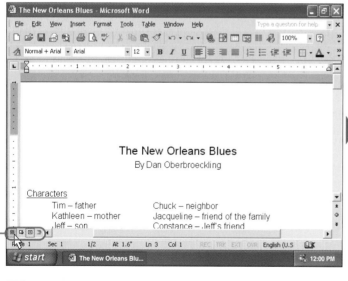

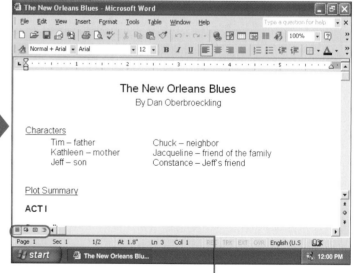

1 To change the view of your document, click one of the following buttons.

- ▤ Normal
- ▣ Web Layout
- ▣ Print Layout
- ▤ Outline

■ Your document appears in the view you selected.

■ A blue border appears around the button for the view you selected.

THE DOCUMENT VIEWS

Normal View

The Normal view simplifies the layout of your document so you can quickly enter, edit and format text. This view does not display certain elements in your document, such as margins, headers, footers, page numbers and some types of graphics.

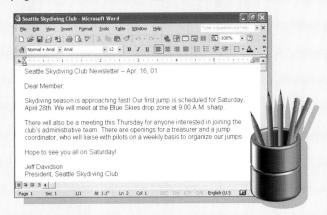

Web Layout View

Working in the Web Layout view is useful when you are creating a Web page or a document that you plan to view only on a computer screen.

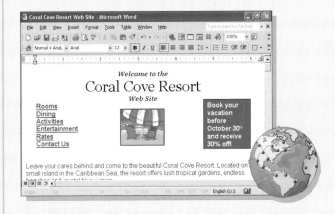

Print Layout View

You can work in the Print Layout view when you want to see how your document will appear on a printed page. This view displays all elements in your document, such as margins, headers, footers, page numbers and graphics.

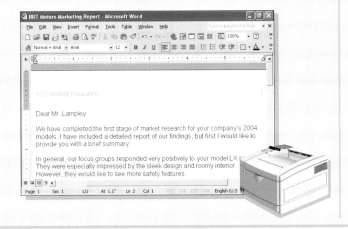

Outline View

The Outline view is useful when you want to review and work with the structure of your document. This view allows you to collapse a document to see only the headings or expand a document to see all the headings and text. The Outline view is useful when working with long documents.

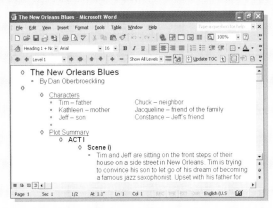

DISPLAY OR HIDE THE RULER

You can display or hide the ruler at any time. The ruler helps you position text in a document.

When you first start Word, the ruler appears on your screen.

You cannot display or hide the ruler in the Outline view. For information on the views, see page 36.

DISPLAY OR HIDE THE RULER

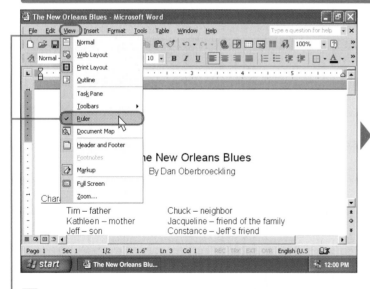

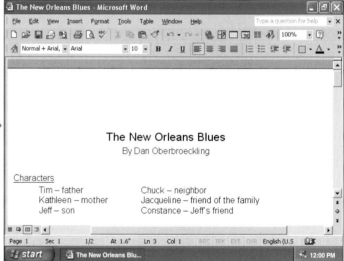

1 Click **View**.

2 Click **Ruler**. A check mark (✔) beside Ruler indicates the ruler is currently displayed.

Note: If Ruler does not appear on the menu, position the mouse ⏳ over the bottom of the menu to display all the menu options.

■ Word displays or hides the ruler.

Note: Hiding the ruler provides a larger and less cluttered working area.

> Word offers several toolbars that you can display or hide to suit your needs. Toolbars contain buttons that you can select to quickly perform common tasks.

When you first start Word, the **Standard** and **Formatting** toolbars appear on your screen.

DISPLAY OR HIDE A TOOLBAR

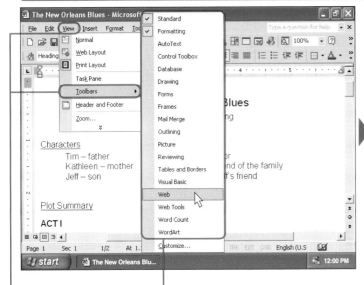

1 Click **View**.

2 Click **Toolbars**.

■ A list of toolbars appears. A check mark (✔) appears beside the name of each toolbar that is currently displayed.

3 Click the name of the toolbar you want to display or hide.

■ Word displays or hides the toolbar you selected.

Note: A screen displaying fewer toolbars provides a larger and less cluttered working area.

39

You can
move a toolbar
to the top, bottom,
right or left edge
of your screen.

You can move
a toolbar to the
same row as
another toolbar
or to its own row.

MOVE A TOOLBAR

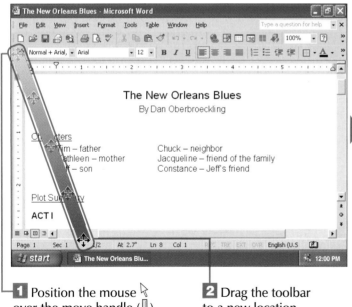

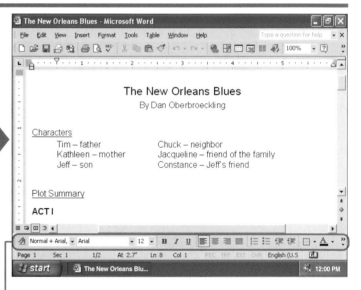

1 Position the mouse ⇧ over the move handle (▐) of the toolbar you want to move (⇧ changes to ✛).

2 Drag the toolbar to a new location.

■ The toolbar appears in the new location.

SIZE A TOOLBAR

You can increase the size of a toolbar to display more buttons on the toolbar. This is useful when a toolbar appears on the same row as another toolbar and cannot display all of its buttons.

You cannot size a toolbar that appears on its own row.

SIZE A TOOLBAR

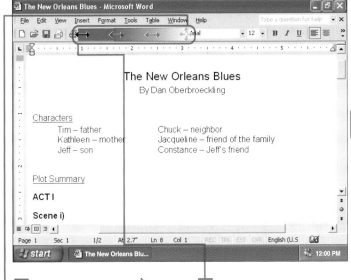

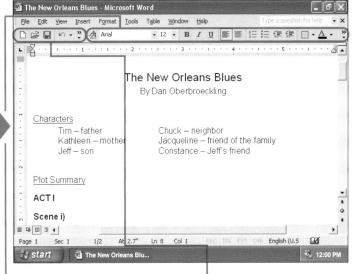

1 Position the mouse ⌖ over the move handle (⫴) of the toolbar you want to size (⌖ changes to ✛).

2 Drag the mouse ↔ until the toolbar is the size you want.

■ The toolbar displays the new size.

■ The new toolbar size affects the location and size of other toolbars on the same row.

You can increase the zoom setting to view an area of your document in more detail or decrease the zoom setting to view more of your document at once.

The available zoom settings depend on the current view of your document. For information on the views, see page 36.

ZOOM IN OR OUT

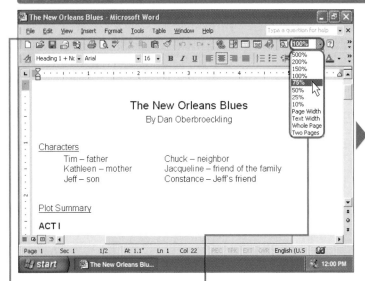

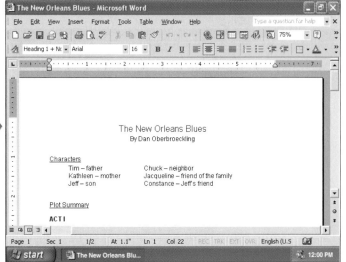

1 Click ☐ in this area to display a list of zoom settings.

Note: If the Zoom area is not displayed, click ☒ on the Standard toolbar to display the area.

2 Click the zoom setting you want to use.

*Note: Select **Page Width** or **Text Width** to fit the page or the text across the width of your screen. Select **Whole Page** or **Two Pages** to display one or two full pages across your screen.*

■ The document appears in the new zoom setting. You can edit the document as usual.

■ Changing the zoom setting will not affect the way text appears on a printed page.

■ To return to the normal zoom setting, repeat steps **1** and **2**, selecting **100%** in step **2**.

DISPLAY OR HIDE WHITE SPACE

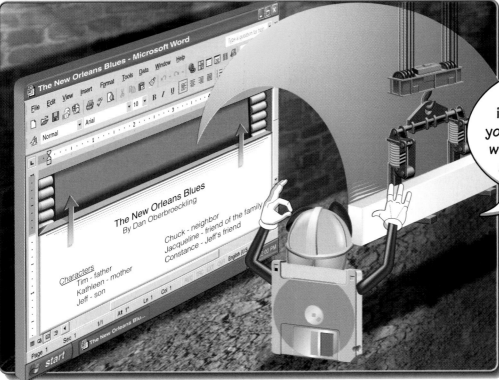

When your document is displayed in the Print Layout view, you can display or hide the white space that appears at the top and bottom of each page.

Hiding the white space allows you to display more text on your screen at once.

DISPLAY OR HIDE WHITE SPACE

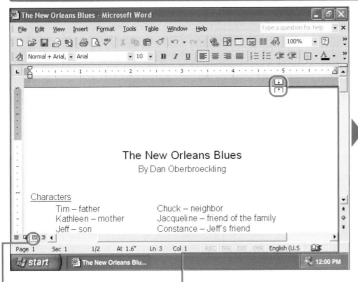

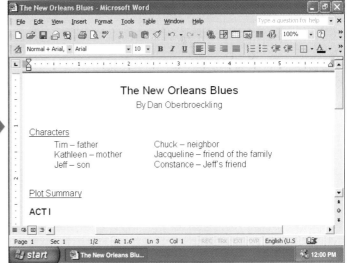

1 Click 🔲 to display your document in the Print Layout view.

2 Position the mouse I over the top or bottom edge of a page (I changes to ⊬ or ⊭).

3 Click the edge of the page to display or hide the white space.

■ Word displays or hides the white space on each page.

Note: If the document contains more than one page, Word also displays or hides the gray space between the pages.

CHAPTER 4

EDIT TEXT

Do you want to edit the text in your document or check your document for spelling and grammar errors? This chapter teaches you how.

INSERT TEXT

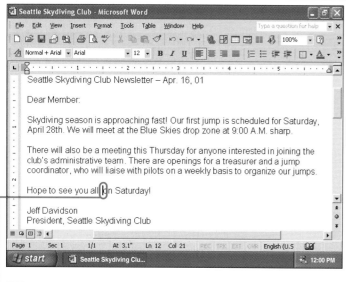

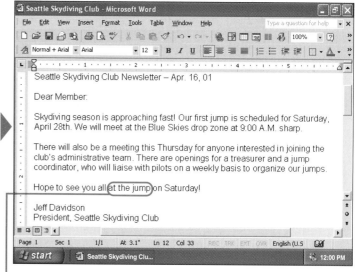

1 Click the location in your document where you want to insert new text.

■ The text you type will appear where the insertion point flashes on your screen.

Note: You can press the ← , → , ↑ or ↓ key to move the insertion point one character or line in any direction.

2 Type the text you want to insert.

■ To insert a blank space, press the **Spacebar**.

■ The words to the right of the new text move forward.

Why does the existing text in my document disappear when I insert new text?

If the text you type replaces existing text in your document, you may have turned on the Overtype feature. When the Overtype feature is turned on, the **OVR** status indicator at the bottom of your screen is **bold**. To turn the Overtype feature on or off, press the Insert key.

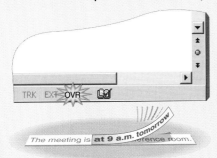

Why did red and green underlines appear under the text I inserted?

Word automatically checks your document for spelling and grammar errors as you type. Misspelled words display a red underline and grammar errors display a green underline. For information on checking spelling and grammar in your document, see page 58.

DELETE TEXT

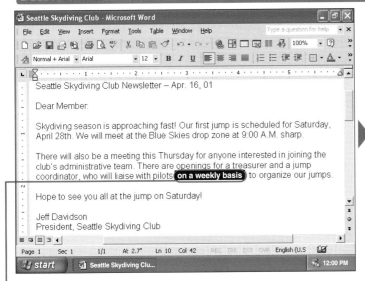

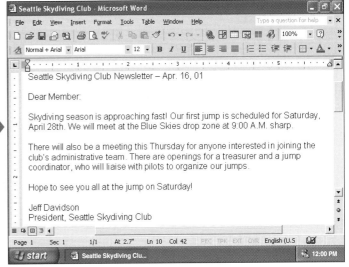

1 Select the text you want to delete. To select text, see page 10.

2 Press the Delete key to remove the text.

■ The text disappears. The remaining text in the line or paragraph moves to fill the empty space.

■ To delete a single character, click to the right of the character you want to delete and then press the ◆Backspace key. Word deletes the character to the left of the flashing insertion point.

MOVE OR COPY TEXT

You can move or copy text to a new location in your document.

Moving text allows you to rearrange text in your document. When you move text, the text disappears from its original location.

Copying text allows you to repeat information in your document without having to retype the text. When you copy text, the text appears in both the original and new locations.

MOVE OR COPY TEXT

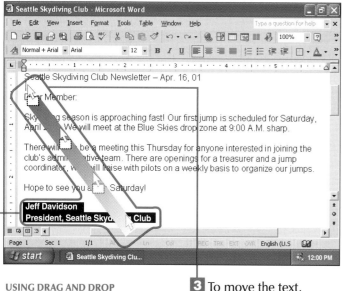

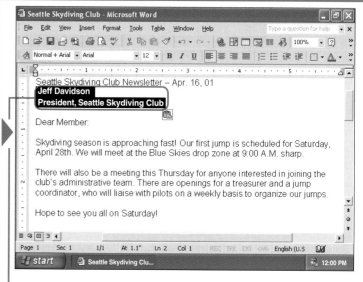

USING DRAG AND DROP

1 Select the text you want to move. To select text, see page 10.

2 Position the mouse I over the selected text (I changes to ⬚).

3 To move the text, drag the mouse ⬚ to the location where you want to place the text.

Note: The text will appear where you position the dotted insertion point on your screen.

■ The text moves to the new location.

■ To copy text, perform steps **1** to **3**, except press and hold down the Ctrl key as you perform step **3**.

How can I use the Clipboard task pane to move or copy text?

The Clipboard task pane displays up to the last 24 items you have selected to move or copy. To place a clipboard item in your document, click the location where you want the item to appear and then click the item in the task pane. For more information on the task pane, see page 16.

Why does the Paste Options button (📋) appear when I move or copy text?

You can use the Paste Options button (📋) to change the format of text you have moved or copied. For example, you can choose to keep the original formatting of the text or change the formatting of the text to match the text in the new location. Click the Paste Options button to display a list of options and then select the option you want to use. The Paste Options button is available only until you perform another task.

USING THE TOOLBAR BUTTONS

1 Select the text you want to move or copy. To select text, see page 10.

2 Click one of the following buttons.

✂ Move text
📋 Copy text

Note: If the button you want is not displayed, click 》 on the Standard toolbar to display the button.

■ The Clipboard task pane may appear. To use the Clipboard task pane, see the top of this page.

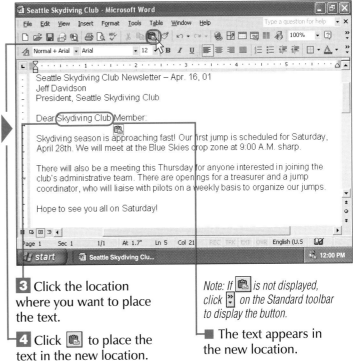

3 Click the location where you want to place the text.

4 Click 📋 to place the text in the new location.

Note: If 📋 is not displayed, click 》 on the Standard toolbar to display the button.

■ The text appears in the new location.

49

INSERT THE DATE AND TIME

> You can insert the current date and time into your document. Word can automatically update the date and time each time you open or print the document.

Word uses your computer's built-in clock to determine the current date and time.

INSERT THE DATE AND TIME

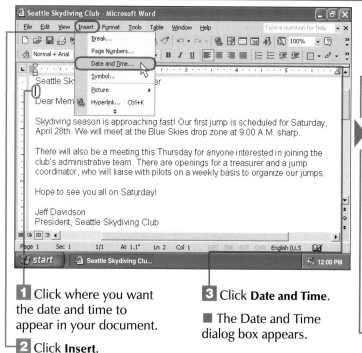

1 Click where you want the date and time to appear in your document.

2 Click **Insert**.

3 Click **Date and Time**.

■ The Date and Time dialog box appears.

4 Click the date and time format you want to use.

5 When this option displays a check mark (✔), Word will automatically update the date and time each time you open or print the document. You can click the option to add (☑) or remove (☐) the check mark.

6 Click **OK** to confirm your selections.

■ The date and time format you selected appears in your document.

50

Word remembers the last changes you made to your document. If you regret these changes, you can cancel them by using the Undo feature.

The Undo feature can cancel your last editing and formatting changes.

UNDO CHANGES

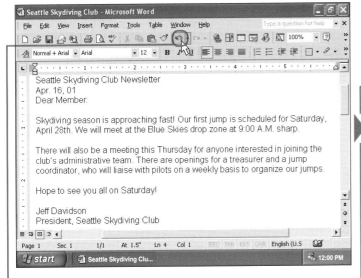

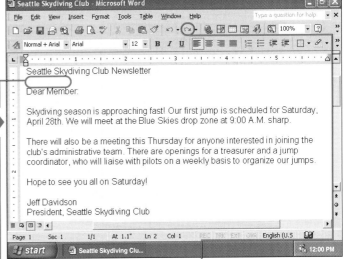

1 Click ⟲ to undo the last change you made to your document.

Note: If ⟲ is not displayed, click ⟩⟩ on the Standard toolbar to display the button.

■ Word cancels the last change you made to your document.

■ You can repeat step **1** to cancel previous changes you made.

■ To reverse the results of using the Undo feature, click ⟳.

Note: If ⟳ is not displayed, click ⟩⟩ on the Standard toolbar to display the button.

Dear Susan:

Trafalgar High School celebrates its 50th anniversary this year. We will be celebrating on September 22nd with an Open House, followed by a buffet dinner.

Please bring your school photos and memorabilia for our display table.

Word Count

You can have Word count the number of words in your document.

When counting the number of words in your document, Word also counts the number of pages, characters, paragraphs and lines in your document.

COUNT WORDS IN A DOCUMENT

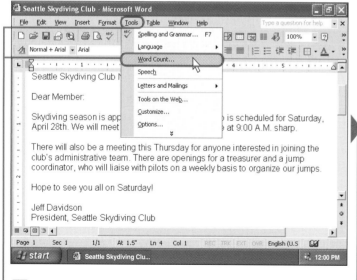

1 Click **Tools**.

2 Click **Word Count**.

■ The Word Count dialog box appears.

■ This area displays the total number of pages, words, characters, paragraphs and lines in your document.

3 When you finish reviewing the information, click **Close** to close the Word Count dialog box.

How can I count the number of words in only part of my document?

To count the number of words in only part of your document, select the text before performing the steps on page 52. To select text, see page 10.

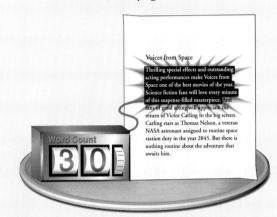

Is there another way to display the Word Count toolbar?

Yes. While reviewing the information in the Word Count dialog box, you can click the **Show Toolbar** button to display the Word Count toolbar.

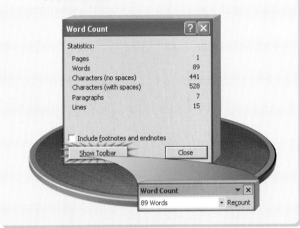

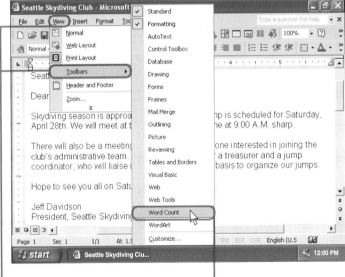

USING THE WORD COUNT TOOLBAR

The Word Count toolbar allows you to quickly recount the number of words in your document as you edit the document.

■1 Click **View**.

■2 Click **Toolbars**.

■3 Click **Word Count**.

■ The Word Count toolbar appears.

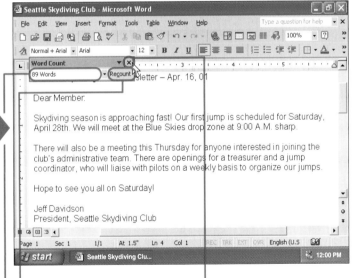

■4 Click **Recount**.

■ This area displays the total number of words in your document.

■ To display the number of characters, lines, pages or paragraphs, you can click this area to select the type of information you want to display.

■5 To update the word count as you edit your document, repeat step 4

■6 When you finish using the Word Count toolbar, click ⊠ to hide the toolbar.

FIND TEXT

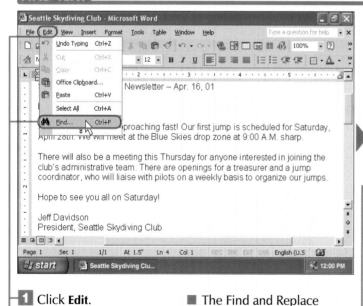

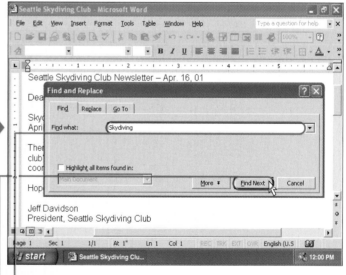

1 Click **Edit**.

2 Click **Find**.

■ The Find and Replace dialog box appears.

3 Type the text you want to find.

4 Click **Find Next** to start the search.

*Note: A dialog box appears if Word cannot find the text you specified. Click **OK** to close the dialog box and then skip to step 8.*

Can I search for part of a word?

When you search for text in your document, Word will find the text even when the text is part of a larger word. For example, if you search for **place**, Word will also find **place**s, **place**ment and common**place**.

places

placement

commonplace

place

Can I search only a specific section of my document?

Yes. To search only a specific section of your document, select the text you want to search before starting the search. To select text, see page 10.

Voices from Space

Thrilling special effects and outstanding acting performances make Voices from Space one of the best movies of the year. Science fiction fans will love every minute of this suspense-filled masterpiece. And fans of good acting will appreciate the return of Victor Carling to the big screen. Carling stars as Thomas Nelson, a veteran NASA astronaut assigned to routine space station duty in the year 2045. But there is nothing routine about the adventure that awaits him.

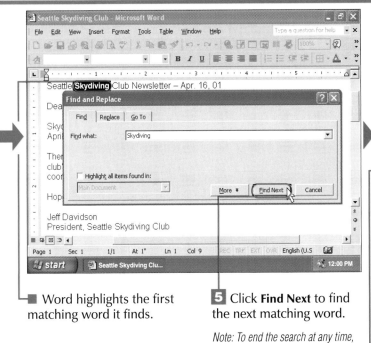

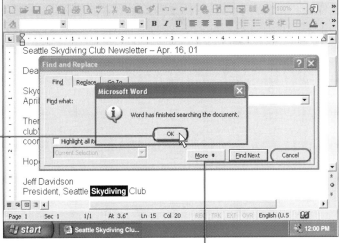

■ Word highlights the first matching word it finds.

5 Click **Find Next** to find the next matching word.

*Note: To end the search at any time, click **Cancel**.*

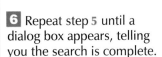

6 Repeat step **5** until a dialog box appears, telling you the search is complete.

7 Click **OK** to close the dialog box.

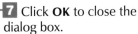

8 Click **Cancel** to close the Find and Replace dialog box.

You can find and replace every occurrence of a word or phrase in your document. This is useful if you have frequently misspelled a name.

REPLACE TEXT

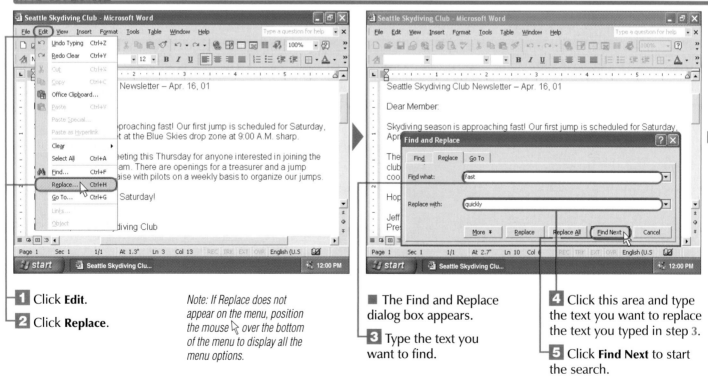

1 Click **Edit**.

2 Click **Replace**.

Note: If Replace does not appear on the menu, position the mouse ⌖ over the bottom of the menu to display all the menu options.

■ The Find and Replace dialog box appears.

3 Type the text you want to find.

4 Click this area and type the text you want to replace the text you typed in step 3.

5 Click **Find Next** to start the search.

Can the Replace feature help me quickly enter text?

Yes. When you need to type a long word or phrase, such as University of Massachusetts, many times in a document, you can use the Replace feature to simplify the task. You can type a short form of the word or phrase, such as UM, throughout your document and then have Word replace the short form with the full word or phrase.

How can I quickly display the Find and Replace dialog box?

You can press and hold down the Ctrl key as you press the H key to quickly display the Find and Replace dialog box.

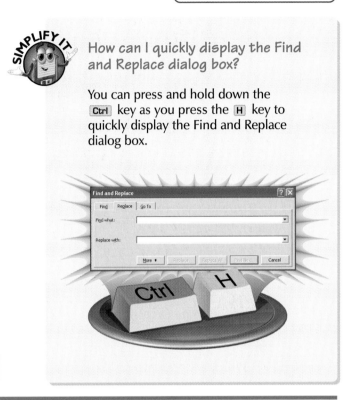

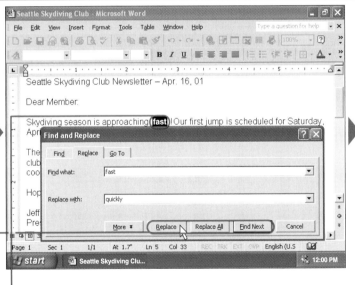

■ Word highlights the first matching word it finds.

6 Click one of the following options.

Replace - Replace the word.

Replace All - Replace all occurrences of the word in the document.

Find Next - Ignore the word.

Note: To cancel the search at any time, press the Esc key.

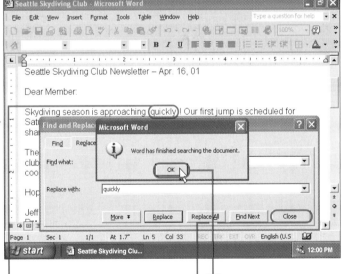

■ In this example, Word replaces the word and searches for the next matching word.

7 Replace or ignore matching words until a dialog box appears, telling you the search is complete.

8 Click **OK** to close the dialog box.

9 Click **Close** or **Cancel** to close the Find and Replace dialog box.

CHECK SPELLING AND GRAMMAR

You can find and correct all the spelling and grammar errors in your document.

Spelling Error:
wether

Suggestions
weather
wetter
whether
wither

Grammar Error:
I did not buy no books.

I did not buy any books.

Word compares every word in your document to words in its dictionary. If a word does not exist in the dictionary, the word is considered misspelled.

Word will not find a correctly spelled word used in the wrong context, such as "My niece is **sit** years old." You should carefully review your document to find this type of error.

CHECK SPELLING AND GRAMMAR

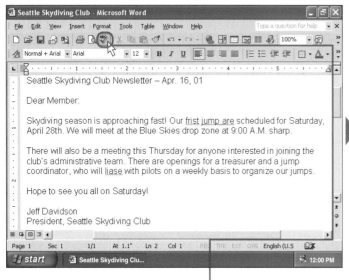

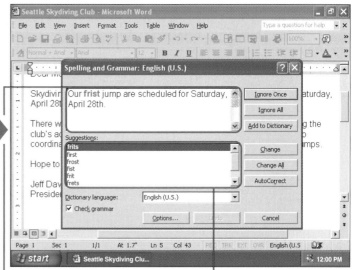

■ Word automatically underlines misspelled words in red and grammar errors in green. The underlines will not appear when you print your document.

1 Click to check your document for spelling and grammar errors.

Note: If is not displayed, click on the Standard toolbar to display the button.

■ The Spelling and Grammar dialog box appears if Word finds an error in your document.

■ This area displays the first misspelled word or grammar error.

■ This area displays suggestions for correcting the error.

58

Can Word automatically correct my typing mistakes?

Yes. Word automatically corrects common spelling errors as you type. To view a complete list of the spelling errors that Word will automatically correct, see page 62.

adn	and
alot	a lot
comittee	committee
don;t	don't
nwe	new
occurence	occurrence
recieve	receive
seperate	separate
teh	the

How can I quickly correct a single misspelled word or grammar error in my document?

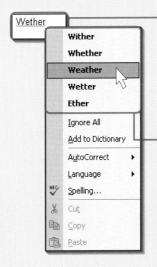

1 Right-click the misspelled word or grammar error in your document.

■ A menu appears with suggestions to correct the error.

2 Click the suggestion you want to use to correct the error.

Note: If you do not want to use any of the suggestions, click outside the menu to close the menu.

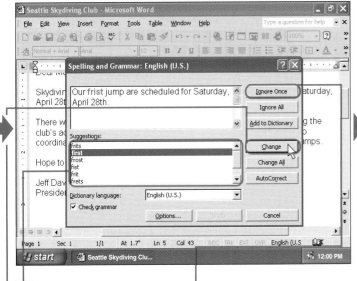

2 Click the suggestion you want to use to correct the error.

3 Click **Change** to correct the error in your document.

■ To skip the error and continue checking your document, click **Ignore Once**.

*Note: To skip the error and all other occurrences of the error in your document, click **Ignore All** or **Ignore Rule**. The name of the button depends on whether the error is a misspelled word or a grammar error.*

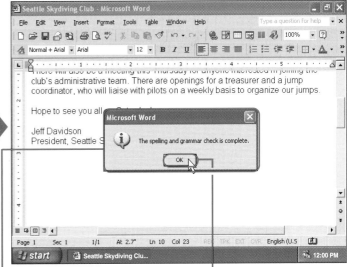

4 Correct or ignore misspelled words and grammar errors until this dialog box appears, telling you the spelling and grammar check is complete.

5 Click **OK** to close the dialog box.

You can use the thesaurus to replace a word in your document with a more suitable word.

Word **Suggestions**

The thesaurus can replace a word in your document with a word that shares the same meaning, called a synonym.

Using the thesaurus included with Word is faster and more convenient than searching through a printed thesaurus.

USING THE THESAURUS

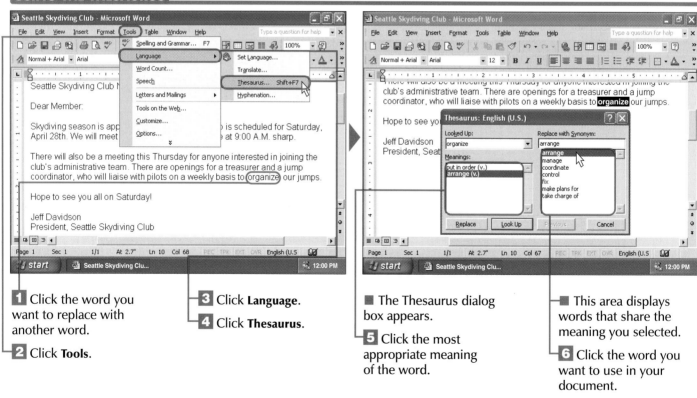

1 Click the word you want to replace with another word.

2 Click **Tools**.

3 Click **Language**.

4 Click **Thesaurus**.

■ The Thesaurus dialog box appears.

5 Click the most appropriate meaning of the word.

■ This area displays words that share the meaning you selected.

6 Click the word you want to use in your document.

Why would I use the thesaurus?

Many people use the thesaurus to replace a word that appears repeatedly in a document. Replacing repeatedly used words can help add variety to your writing and make your document appear more professional. You may also want to use the thesaurus to find a word that more clearly explains a concept.

What if the Thesaurus dialog box does not display a word I want to use?

You can look up synonyms for the words displayed in the Thesaurus dialog box to find a more suitable word.

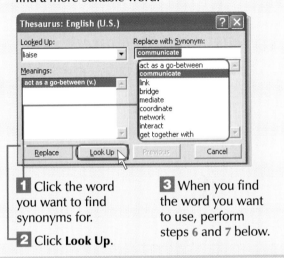

1 Click the word you want to find synonyms for.

2 Click **Look Up**.

3 When you find the word you want to use, perform steps **6** and **7** below.

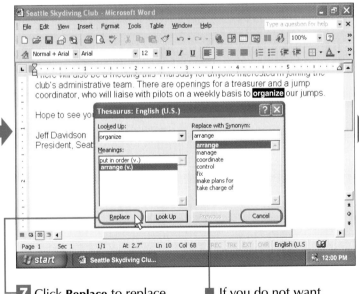

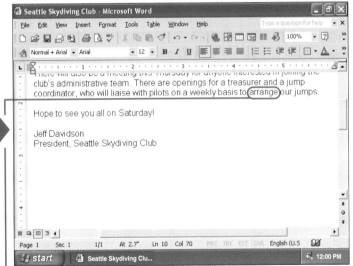

7 Click **Replace** to replace the word in your document with the word you selected.

■ If you do not want to use any of the words displayed in the Thesaurus dialog box, click **Cancel** to close the dialog box.

■ The word you selected replaces the word in your document.

USING AUTOCORRECT

Word automatically corrects hundreds of typing and spelling errors as you type. You can create an AutoCorrect entry to add your own word or phrase to the list of errors that Word corrects.

(c)	©
(tm)	TM
accordingto	according to
ahve	have
can;t	can't
i	I
may of been	may have been
recieve	receive
seperate	separate
teh	the

USING AUTOCORRECT

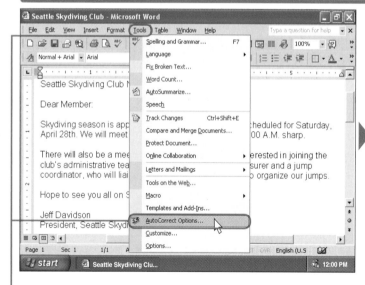

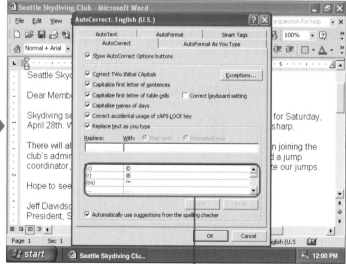

1 Click **Tools**.

2 Click **AutoCorrect Options**.

Note: If AutoCorrect Options does not appear on the menu, position the mouse ⌖ over the bottom of the menu to display all the menu options.

■ The AutoCorrect dialog box appears.

■ This area displays the list of AutoCorrect entries included with Word.

What other types of errors does Word automatically correct?

When you type two consecutive uppercase letters, Word automatically converts the second letter to lowercase. When you type a lowercase letter for the first letter of a sentence or the name of a day, Word automatically converts the letter to uppercase.

Error		Correction
PRinter	⟹	Printer
friday	⟹	Friday
today I went to the dentist.	⟹	Today I went to the dentist.

Why does a blue rectangle (▬) appear when I position the mouse I over a word in my document?

A blue rectangle appears below a word that has been automatically corrected.

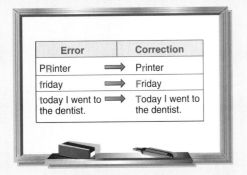

1 If you do not want to accept the correction, position the mouse I over the blue rectangle to display the AutoCorrect Options button (🔁).

2 Click the AutoCorrect Options button to display a list of options for the correction.

3 Click the option you want to use.

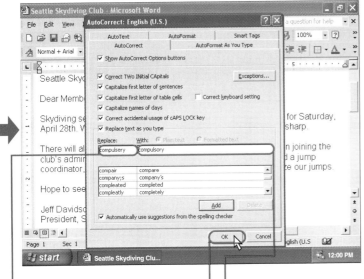

3 To add a new entry to the list, type the text you want Word to replace automatically. The text should not contain spaces and should not be a real word.

4 Click this area and type the text you want Word to automatically insert into your documents.

5 Click **OK** to confirm your change.

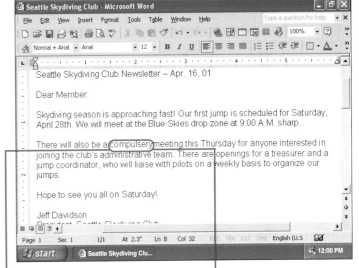

INSERT AN AUTOCORRECT ENTRY

■ After you create an AutoCorrect entry, Word will automatically insert the entry each time you type the corresponding text.

1 Click the location where you want the AutoCorrect entry to appear.

2 Type the text Word will automatically replace.

3 Press the **Spacebar** and Word automatically replaces the text with the AutoCorrect entry.

USING AUTOTEXT

You can use the AutoText feature to store text you frequently use, such as a mailing address, legal disclaimer or closing remark. You can then insert the text into your documents.

MEMO

ATTENTION: Lindsay Sandman
FROM: Kim Johnson
DATE: February 20, 2002

This memo is a reminder of our meeting with the President of ABC Incorporated tomorrow morning. We will be presenting our advertising campaign and reviewing the sales figures from last month. Lunch will be served after the meeting.

Thank you for your help with this presentaion.

Kim Johnson
Project Manager
ABC Inc.

Using the AutoText feature saves you from having to type the same information over and over.

USING AUTOTEXT

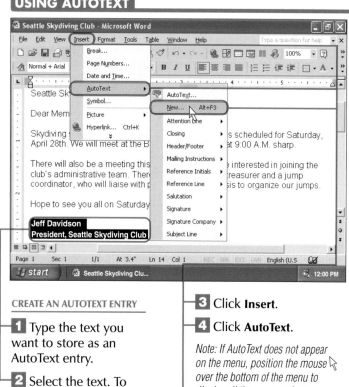

CREATE AN AUTOTEXT ENTRY

1 Type the text you want to store as an AutoText entry.

2 Select the text. To select text, see page 10.

3 Click **Insert**.

4 Click **AutoText**.

Note: If AutoText does not appear on the menu, position the mouse over the bottom of the menu to display all the menu options.

5 Click **New**.

■ The Create AutoText dialog box appears.

6 This area displays a name for the AutoText entry. To use a different name, type the name.

Note: The name of an AutoText entry should be at least four characters long.

7 Click **OK** to create the AutoText entry.

Does Word come with any AutoText entries?

Word comes with AutoText entries that can help you quickly create a letter.

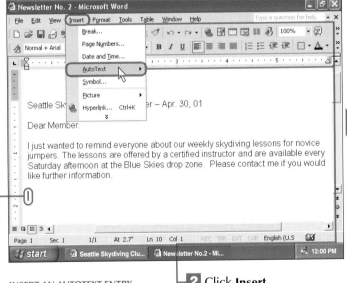

How can I quickly insert an AutoText entry into my document?

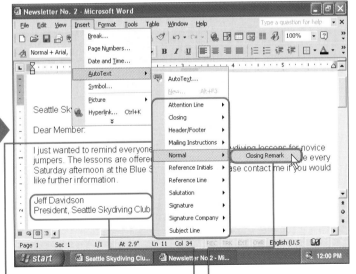

1 To quickly insert an AutoText entry, type the first few characters of the name of the AutoText entry.

■ A yellow box appears, displaying the AutoText entry for the text you typed.

2 To insert the AutoText entry, press the **Enter** key.

■ To ignore the AutoText entry, continue typing.

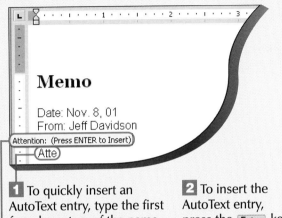

INSERT AN AUTOTEXT ENTRY

1 Click where you want the AutoText entry to appear in your document.

2 Click **Insert**.

3 Click **AutoText**.

Note: If AutoText does not appear on the menu, position the mouse ⌖ over the bottom of the menu to display all the menu options.

4 Click the category that stores the AutoText entry you want to use.

Note: The Normal category stores most AutoText entries you have created.

5 Click the AutoText entry you want to use.

■ The text appears in your document.

INSERT SYMBOLS

INSERT SYMBOLS

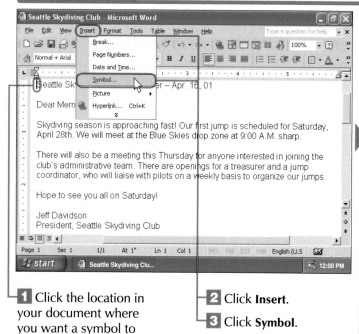

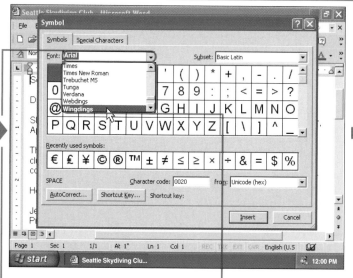

1 Click the location in your document where you want a symbol to appear.

2 Click **Insert**.

3 Click **Symbol**.

■ The Symbol dialog box appears, displaying the symbols for the current font.

4 To display the symbols for another font, click ▾ in this area.

5 Click the font that provides the symbols you want to display.

How can I quickly insert a symbol I recently used?

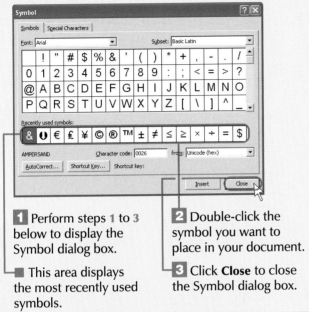

1 Perform steps **1** to **3** below to display the Symbol dialog box.

■ This area displays the most recently used symbols.

2 Double-click the symbol you want to place in your document.

3 Click **Close** to close the Symbol dialog box.

Is there another way to enter symbols in my document?

When you type one of the following sets of characters, Word automatically replaces the characters with a symbol.

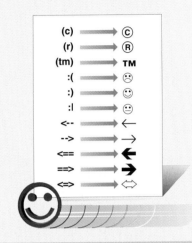

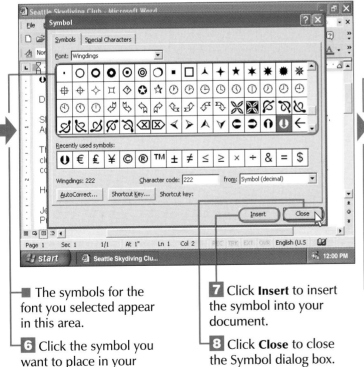

■ The symbols for the font you selected appear in this area.

6 Click the symbol you want to place in your document.

7 Click **Insert** to insert the symbol into your document.

8 Click **Close** to close the Symbol dialog box.

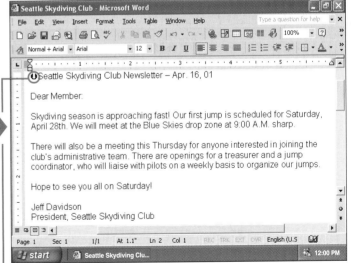

■ The symbol appears in your document.

■ To remove a symbol from your document, drag the mouse I over the symbol until you highlight the symbol and then press the Delete key.

USING SMART TAGS

Word labels certain types of information, such as dates and addresses, with smart tags. You can use a smart tag to perform an action, such as scheduling a meeting on a specific date or displaying a map for an address.

USING SMART TAGS

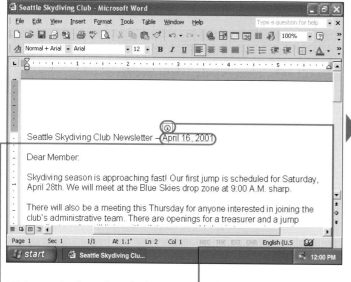

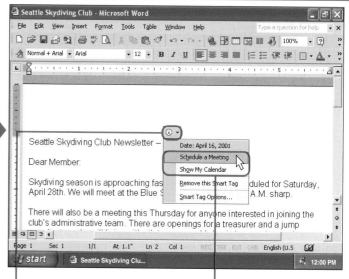

■ A purple dotted underline appears below text Word labels with a smart tag.

1 To perform an action using a smart tag, position the mouse I over the text labeled with a smart tag.

■ The Smart Tag Actions button appears.

2 Click the Smart Tag Actions button to display a list of actions you can perform using the smart tag.

3 Click the action you want to perform.

■ The program that allows you to perform the action will appear on your screen.

Can I remove a smart tag from my document?

Yes. To remove a smart tag from text in your document, perform steps 1 to 3 on page 68, selecting **Remove this Smart Tag** in step 3.

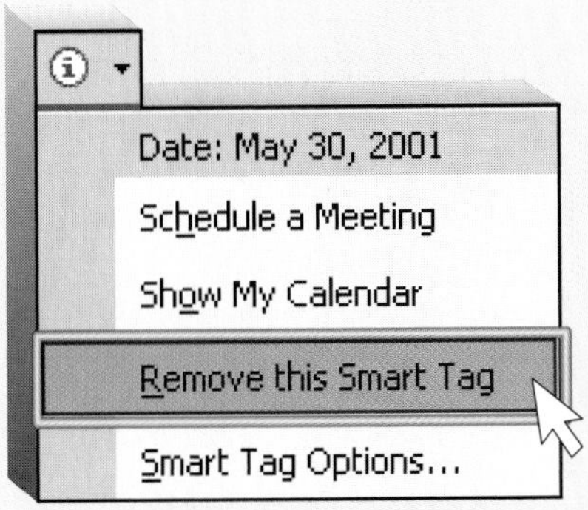

What types of information can Word label with smart tags?

Word can label people's names, dates, times, addresses, places and telephone numbers with smart tags. Word can also label e-mail addresses of people you recently sent messages to using Microsoft Outlook and financial symbols you type in capital letters, such as MSFT.

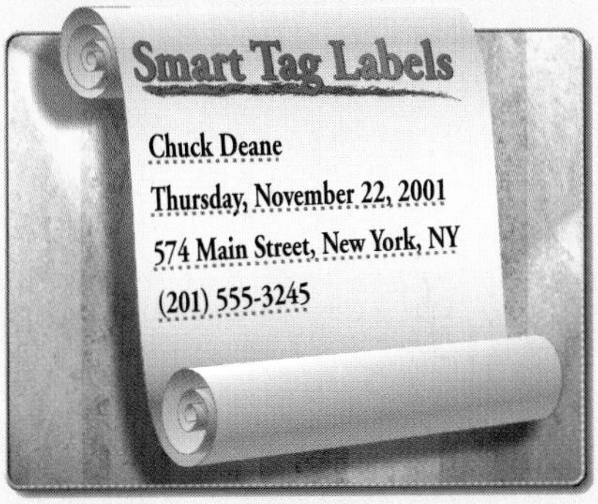

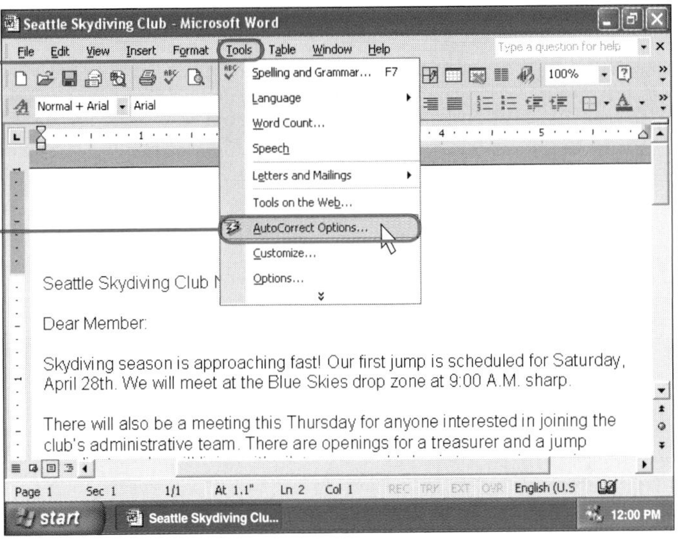

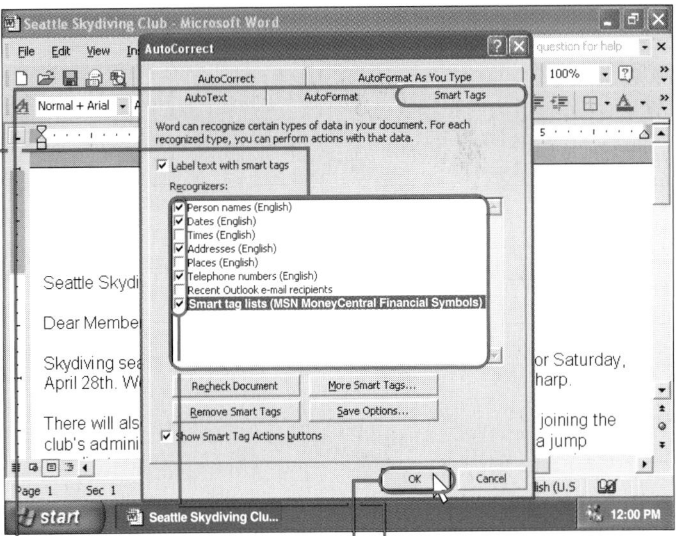

CHANGE SMART TAG OPTIONS

1 Click **Tools**.

2 Click **AutoCorrect Options**.

Note: If AutoCorrect Options does not appear on the menu, position the mouse over the bottom of the menu to display all the menu options.

■ The AutoCorrect dialog box appears.

3 Click the **Smart Tags** tab.

■ This area displays the types of information Word can label with smart tags. Smart tags are turned on for each type of information that displays a check mark (✔).

4 You can click the box beside a type of information to turn smart tags on (☑) or off (☐) for the information.

5 Click **OK** to confirm your changes.

ADD A COMMENT

You can add a comment to text in your document. A comment can be a note, explanation or reminder about information you need to verify later.

Comment: Verify date

ADD A COMMENT

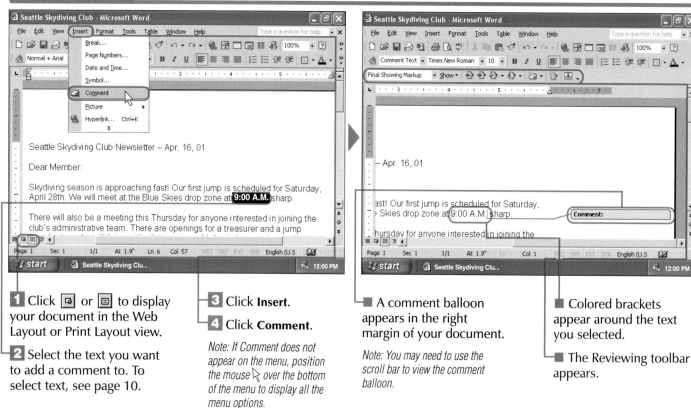

1 Click 🔲 or 🔲 to display your document in the Web Layout or Print Layout view.

2 Select the text you want to add a comment to. To select text, see page 10.

3 Click **Insert**.

4 Click **Comment**.

Note: If Comment does not appear on the menu, position the mouse ⌨ over the bottom of the menu to display all the menu options.

■ A comment balloon appears in the right margin of your document.

Note: You may need to use the scroll bar to view the comment balloon.

■ Colored brackets appear around the text you selected.

■ The Reviewing toolbar appears.

Can I edit a comment?

You can edit a comment to update the information in the comment. Click the comment balloon containing the comment you want to edit. You can then edit the text as you would edit any text in a document. To edit text, see page 46.

Comment: Verify date

How do I view a comment in the Normal or Outline view?

In the Normal and Outline view, colored brackets appear around text you have added a comment to. To view a comment, position the mouse I over the text for the comment. After a few seconds, the comment will appear in a colored box. For more information on the views, see page 36.

Jeff, 9/22/2001 12:00 PM:
Commented - Confirm time with pilot.

is sche
at 9:00 A.M. sharp.

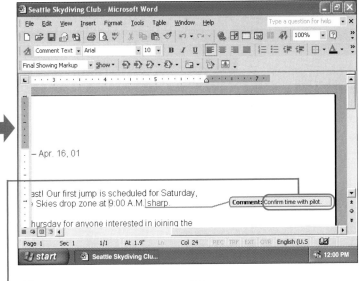

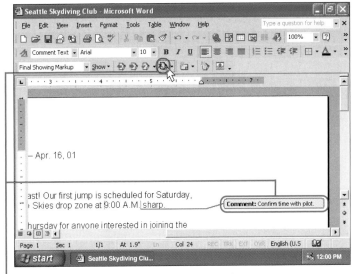

5 Type the comment you want to add.

6 When you finish typing the comment, click outside the comment balloon.

DELETE A COMMENT

1 Click the comment balloon containing the comment you want to delete.

2 Click 🗑 to delete the comment.

■ Word deletes the comment and removes the comment balloon and colored brackets from your document.

■ When you finish working with your comments, you can hide the Reviewing toolbar. To hide a toolbar, see page 39.

TRACK CHANGES

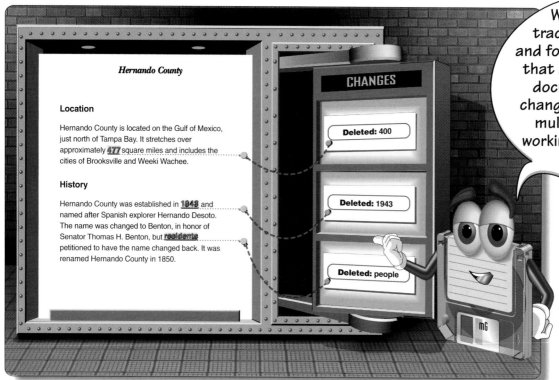

Word can keep track of the editing and formatting changes that are made to your document. Tracking changes is useful when multiple people are working with the same document.

Multiple people can work with a document you store on your network. Word will keep track of the changes you make to the document, as well as the changes that other people make.

TRACK CHANGES

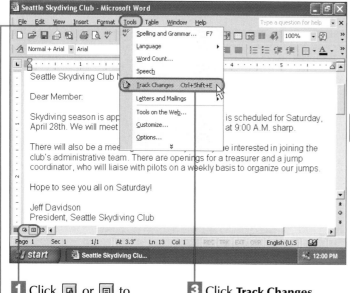

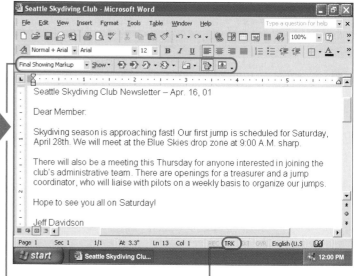

1 Click ▣ or ▤ to display the document in the Web Layout or Print Layout view.

2 Click **Tools**.

3 Click **Track Changes**.

Note: If Track Changes does not appear on the menu, position the mouse ⊳ over the bottom of the menu to display all the menu options.

■ The Reviewing toolbar appears.

■ When Word tracks changes, this area displays **TRK** in bold.

4 You can now make changes to the document you want Word to track.

The balloons do not appear in the margin of the document. What is wrong?

The balloons only appear in the margin of a document when the document is displayed in the Print Layout or Web Layout view. When the document is displayed in the Normal or Outline view, deleted text appears in the body of the document, crossed out and in color. Formatted text displays the formatting. For information on the views, see page 36.

- ✓ PRINT LAYOUT
- ✓ WEB LAYOUT

Will the tracked changes appear on a printed page?

Yes. When you print a document that displays tracked changes, Word may automatically shrink the text in the document to fit the tracked changes on the printed page.

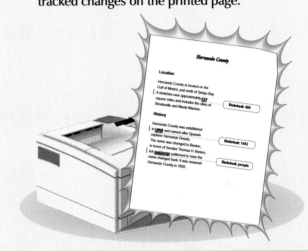

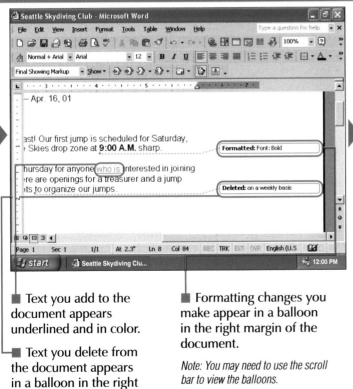

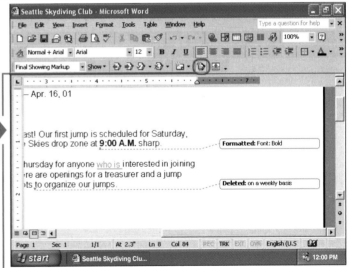

■ Text you add to the document appears underlined and in color.

■ Text you delete from the document appears in a balloon in the right margin of the document.

■ Formatting changes you make appear in a balloon in the right margin of the document.

Note: You may need to use the scroll bar to view the balloons.

■ A vertical line appears in the left margin beside text that contains a tracked change.

■ To stop tracking changes in the document, click 🖹.

■ You can now review the tracked changes in the document. To review tracked changes, see page 74.

REVIEW TRACKED CHANGES

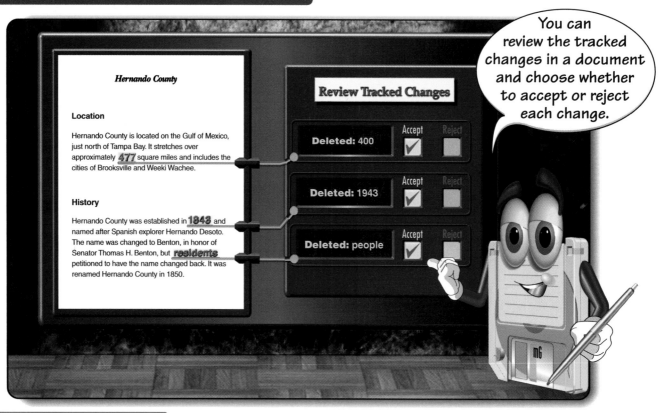

You can review the tracked changes in a document and choose whether to accept or reject each change.

REVIEW TRACKED CHANGES

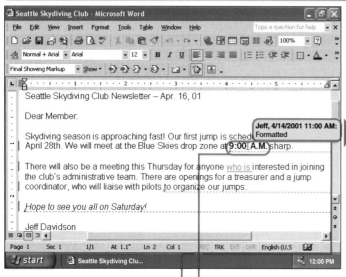

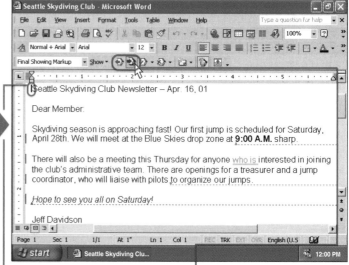

1 Open the document you want to review tracked changes for. To open a document, see page 26.

■ Word displays the changes that each person made in a different color.

2 To display information about a change, position the mouse I over the change.

■ After a few seconds, a colored box appears, displaying the name of the person who made the change and the date and time the change was made.

3 Click at the beginning of the document.

4 Click one of the following buttons to move to a tracked change in the document.

🔁 Previous

🔁 Next

How can I accept all the changes in a document at once?

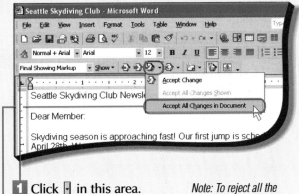

1 Click ⊡ in this area.

2 Click **Accept All Changes in Document**.

■ Word will accept all the changes in the document and stop tracking the changes.

*Note: To reject all the changes in a document, click ⊡ beside the Reject Change button (🗷) and then click **Reject All Changes in Document**.*

How do I hide the Reviewing toolbar?

You can hide or display the Reviewing toolbar as you would hide or display any toolbar. To hide or display a toolbar, see page 39.

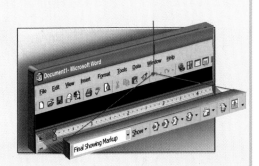

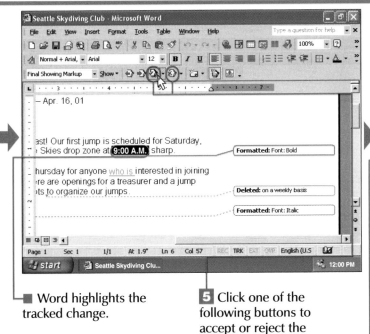

■ Word highlights the tracked change.

5 Click one of the following buttons to accept or reject the change.

🗷 Accept Change
🗷 Reject Change

■ Word accepts or rejects the change and stops tracking the change.

6 Repeat steps 4 and 5 until this dialog box appears.

7 Click **OK** to close the dialog box.

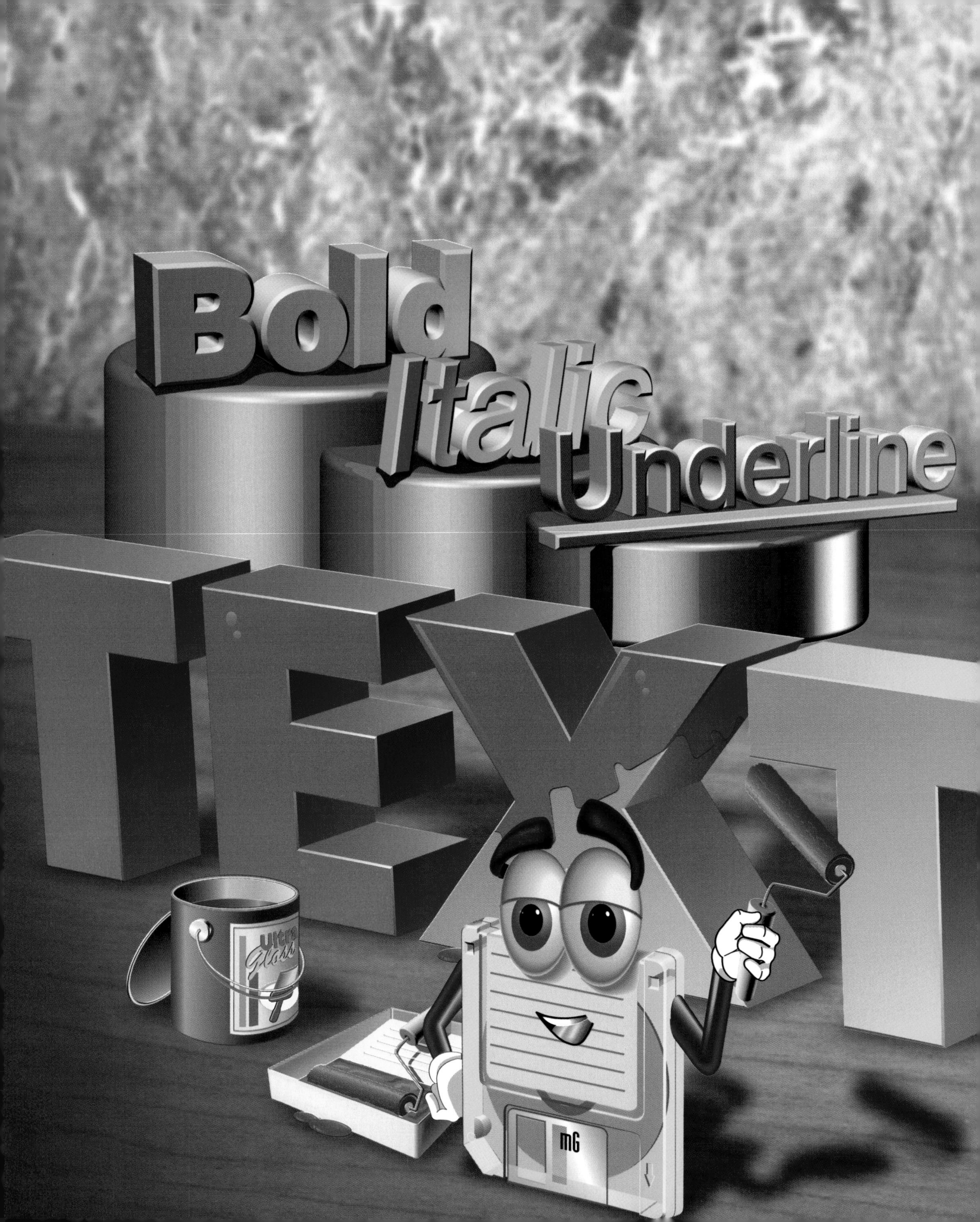
Bold
Italic
Underline
TEXT
Ultra
Gloss
mG

CHAPTER 5

FORMAT TEXT

Would you like to emphasize information in your document and enhance the appearance of text? Read this chapter to learn how.

R MRS. GLEDHILL:
There a 10th anniversary High
School Reunion on August 6, 7
and 8 at Woodblock High
School. We all hope to see you
there. Contact Susan Hughes
for more information.

Maggie Healey

You can change the font of text to enhance the appearance of your document.

CHANGE FONT OF TEXT

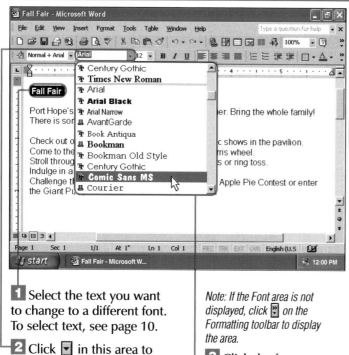

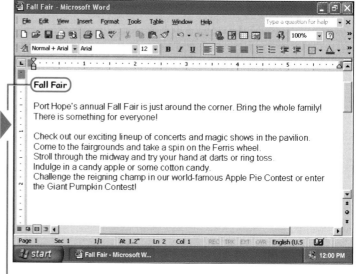

1 Select the text you want to change to a different font. To select text, see page 10.

2 Click ▼ in this area to display a list of the available fonts.

Note: If the Font area is not displayed, click ⟫ on the Formatting toolbar to display the area.

3 Click the font you want to use.

Note: Word displays the fonts you have recently used at the top of the list.

■ The text you selected changes to the new font.

■ To deselect text, click outside the selected area.

CHANGE SIZE OF TEXT

You can increase or decrease the size of text in your document.

Word measures the size of text in points. There are approximately 72 points in one inch.

Larger text is easier to read, but smaller text allows you to fit more information on a page.

CHANGE SIZE OF TEXT

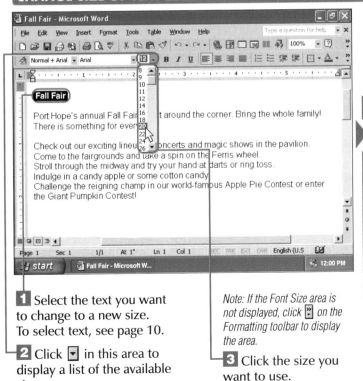

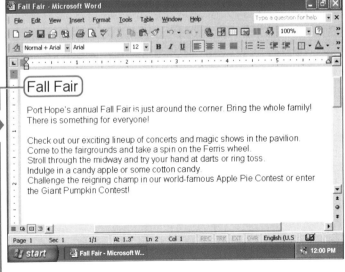

1 Select the text you want to change to a new size. To select text, see page 10.

2 Click ▼ in this area to display a list of the available sizes.

Note: If the Font Size area is not displayed, click ⋙ on the Formatting toolbar to display the area.

3 Click the size you want to use.

■ The text you selected changes to the new size.

■ To deselect text, click outside the selected area.

BOLD, ITALICIZE OR UNDERLINE TEXT

You can bold, italicize or underline text to emphasize information in your document.

BOLD, ITALICIZE OR UNDERLINE TEXT

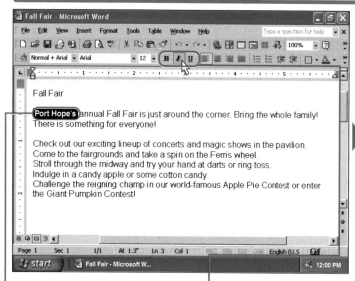

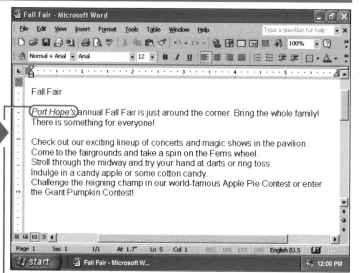

1 Select the text you want to bold, italicize or underline. To select text, see page 10.

2 Click one of the following buttons.

B Bold

I Italic

U Underline

Note: If the button you want is not displayed, click ⁂ on the Formatting toolbar to display the button.

■ The text you selected appears in the new style.

■ To deselect text, click outside the selected area.

■ To remove a bold, italic or underline style, repeat steps 1 and 2.

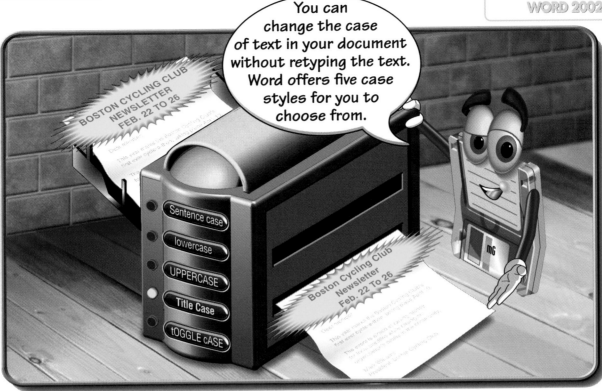

> You can change the case of text in your document without retyping the text. Word offers five case styles for you to choose from.

CHANGE CASE OF TEXT

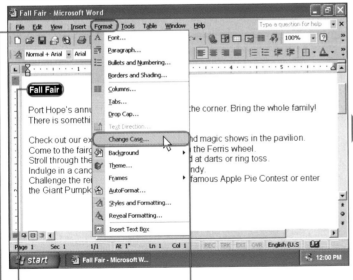

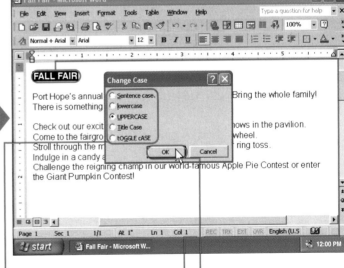

1 Select the text you want to change to a new case style. To select text, see page 10.

2 Click **Format**.

3 Click **Change Case**.

Note: If Change Case does not appear on the menu, position the mouse ⇩ over the bottom of the menu to display all the menu options.

■ The Change Case dialog box appears.

4 Click the case style you want to use (○ changes to ⊙).

5 Click **OK** to confirm your selection.

■ The text you selected changes to the new case style.

■ To deselect text, click outside the selected area.

You can change the color of text to draw attention to headings or important information in your document.

CHANGE COLOR OF TEXT

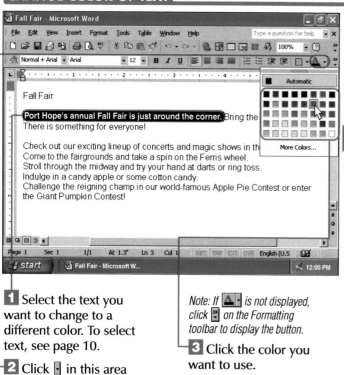

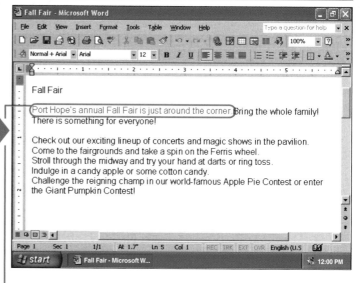

1 Select the text you want to change to a different color. To select text, see page 10.

2 Click ⬝ in this area to display the available colors.

Note: If ▲⬝ is not displayed, click » on the Formatting toolbar to display the button.

3 Click the color you want to use.

■ The text you selected appears in the new color.

■ To deselect text, click outside the selected area.

■ To return text to its original color, repeat steps **1** to **3**, selecting **Automatic** in step **3**.

You can highlight text that you want to stand out in your document. Highlighting text is useful for marking information you want to review or verify later.

If you plan to print your document on a black-and-white printer, use a light highlight color so you will be able to easily read the printed text.

HIGHLIGHT TEXT

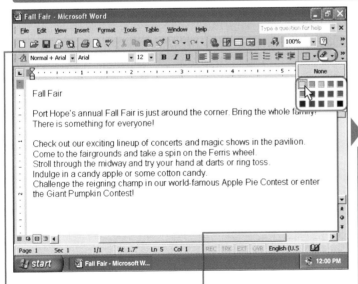

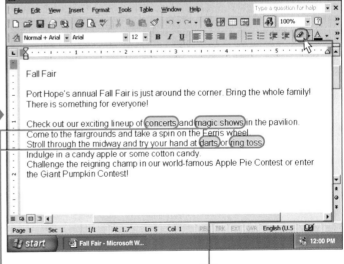

1 Click ⏷ in this area to display the available highlight colors.

Note: If ✏ is not displayed, click ❯ on the Formatting toolbar to display the button.

2 Click the highlight color you want to use.

■ The mouse I changes to ⬧ when over your document.

3 Select each area of text you want to highlight. To select text, see page 10.

■ The text you selected appears highlighted.

4 When you finish highlighting text, click ✏ or press the **Esc** key.

■ To remove a highlight from text, repeat steps **1** to **4**, selecting **None** in step **2**.

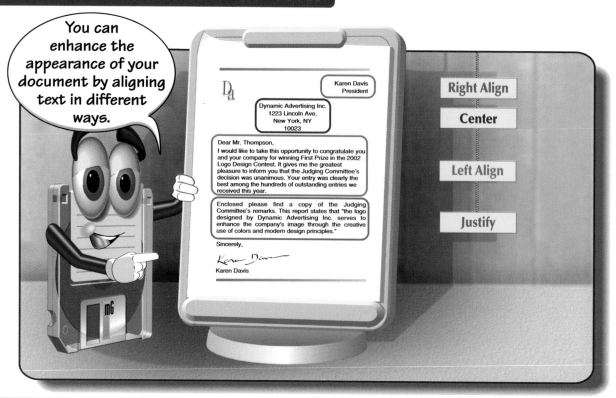

CHANGE ALIGNMENT OF TEXT

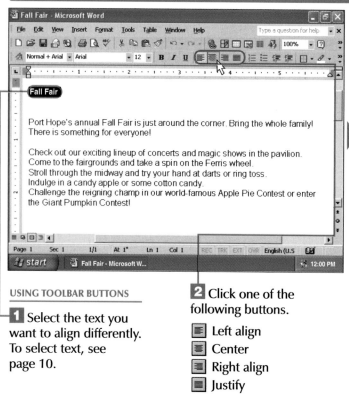

USING TOOLBAR BUTTONS

1 Select the text you want to align differently. To select text, see page 10.

2 Click one of the following buttons.

- Left align
- Center
- Right align
- Justify

Note: If the button you want is not displayed, click >> on the Formatting toolbar to display the button.

■ The text displays the new alignment.

■ To deselect text, click outside the selected area.

Can I use different alignments within a single line of text?

You can use the Click and Type feature to vary the alignment within a line of text. For example, you can left align your name and right align the date on the same line.

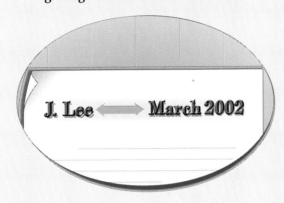

J. Lee ←——→ March 2002

I cannot use the Click and Type feature to align text. What is wrong?

The Click and Type feature is only available in the Web Layout and Print Layout views. To change the view of a document, see page 36.

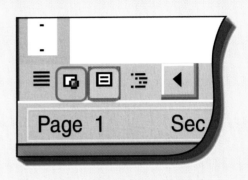

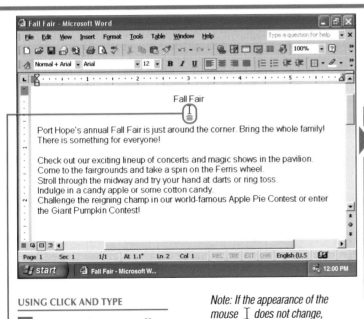

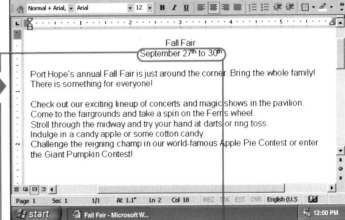

USING CLICK AND TYPE

1 Position the mouse I where you want text to appear. The appearance of the mouse I indicates how Word will align the text.

I⁼ Left align

I Center

⁼I Right align

Note: If the appearance of the mouse I does not change, click where you want to add text.

2 Double-click the location to position the insertion point.

3 Type the text you want to add.

You can make text in your document look more attractive by using various fonts, styles, sizes, effects and colors.

CHANGE APPEARANCE OF TEXT

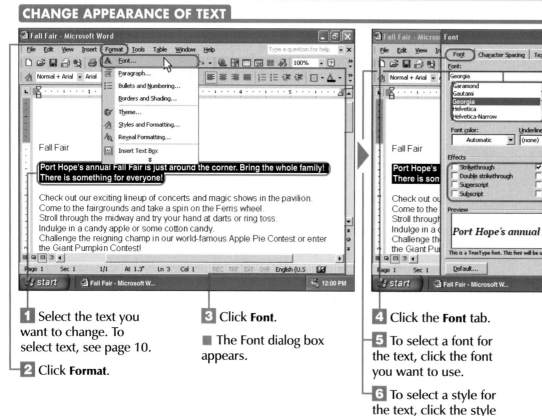

1 Select the text you want to change. To select text, see page 10.

2 Click **Format**.

3 Click **Font**.

■ The Font dialog box appears.

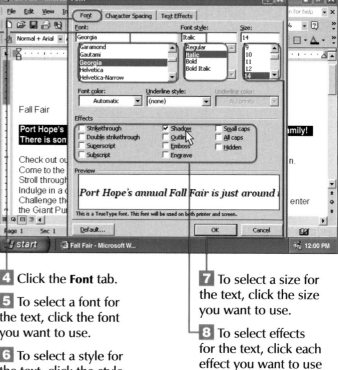

4 Click the **Font** tab.

5 To select a font for the text, click the font you want to use.

6 To select a style for the text, click the style you want to use.

7 To select a size for the text, click the size you want to use.

8 To select effects for the text, click each effect you want to use (□ changes to ☑).

What determines which fonts are available on my computer?

The fonts available on your computer depend on the programs installed on your computer, the setup of your computer and your printer. You can obtain additional fonts at computer stores and on the Internet.

What effects can I add to text in my document?

Word offers many effects that you can use to change the appearance of text in your document.

~~Strikethrough~~
~~Double strikethrough~~
TEXT Superscript
TEXT Subscript
Shadow

Outline
Emboss
Engrave
Sᴍᴀʟʟ Cᴀᴘs
ALL CAPS
Hidden

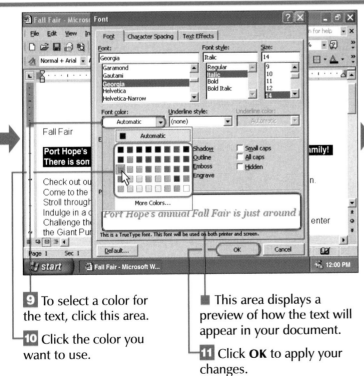

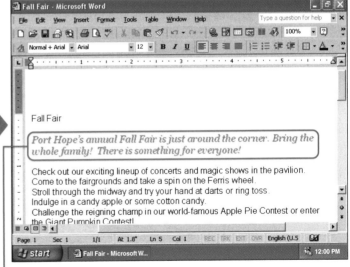

9 To select a color for the text, click this area.

10 Click the color you want to use.

■ This area displays a preview of how the text will appear in your document.

11 Click **OK** to apply your changes.

■ The text you selected displays the changes.

■ To deselect text, click outside the selected area.

COPY FORMATTING

You can copy the formatting of text to make one area of text in your document look exactly like another.

You may want to copy the formatting of text to make all the headings or important words in your document look the same. This will give the text in your document a consistent appearance.

COPY FORMATTING

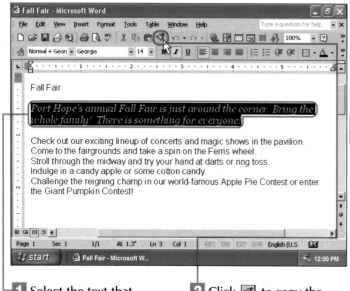

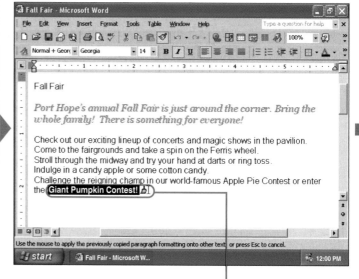

1 Select the text that displays the formatting you want to copy. To select text, see page 10.

2 Click 🖉 to copy the formatting of the text.

Note: If 🖉 is not displayed, click ▾ on the Standard toolbar to display the button.

■ The mouse I changes to ▴I when over your document.

3 Select the text you want to display the formatting.

Will Word copy all the formatting of the original text?

If you copy the formatting of text that contains more than one type of the same formatting, such as multiple fonts, Word will copy only the formatting that appears first. For example, if you select text that contains the Arial font followed by the Monotype Corsiva font, Word will copy only the Arial font.

Arial	Monotype Corsiva

Lindsay *Sandman*

Lindsay Sandman

Arial

Is there another way that I can copy the formatting of text?

Yes. You can use the Styles and Formatting task pane to copy the formatting of text in your document. This task pane lists all the formatting you have applied to text in your document. To use the Styles and Formatting task pane, see page 98.

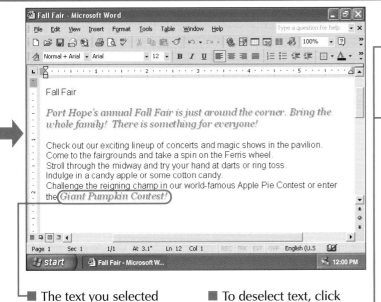

■ The text you selected displays the formatting.

■ To deselect text, click outside the selected area.

COPY FORMATTING TO SEVERAL AREAS

1 Select the text that displays the formatting you want to copy.

2 Double-click 🖌 to copy the formatting of the text.

3 Select each area of text you want to display the formatting.

4 When you finish selecting all the text you want to display the formatting, click 🖌 or press the Esc key.

CHANGE LINE SPACING

You can change the amount of space between the lines of text in your document.

Changing the line spacing can make a document easier to review and edit.

CHANGE LINE SPACING

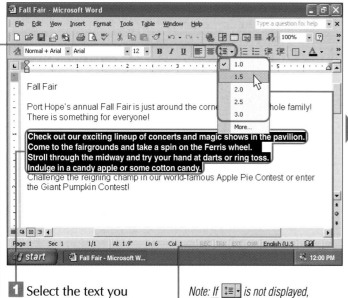

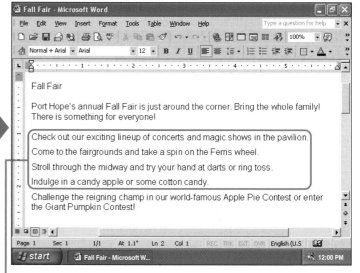

1 Select the text you want to use a different line spacing. To select text, see page 10.

2 Click ⊡ in this area to display the available line spacing options.

Note: If ⧉⊡ *is not displayed, click* ≫ *on the Formatting toolbar to display the button.*

3 Click the line spacing option you want to use.

■ The text appears in the line spacing you selected.

■ To deselect text, click outside the selected area.

You can remove all the formatting you have applied to text in your document.

REMOVE FORMATTING FROM TEXT

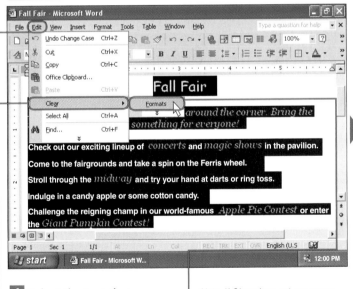

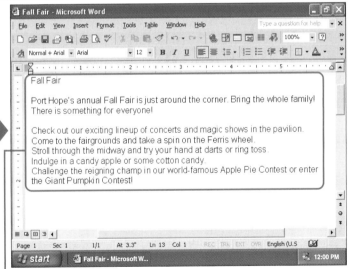

1 Select the text that displays the formatting you want to remove. To select text, see page 10.

2 Click **Edit**.

3 Click **Clear**.

Note: If Clear does not appear on the menu, position the mouse over the bottom of the menu to display all the menu options.

4 Click **Formats**.

■ The formatting disappears from the text.

■ To deselect text, click outside the selected area.

CREATE A BULLETED OR NUMBERED LIST

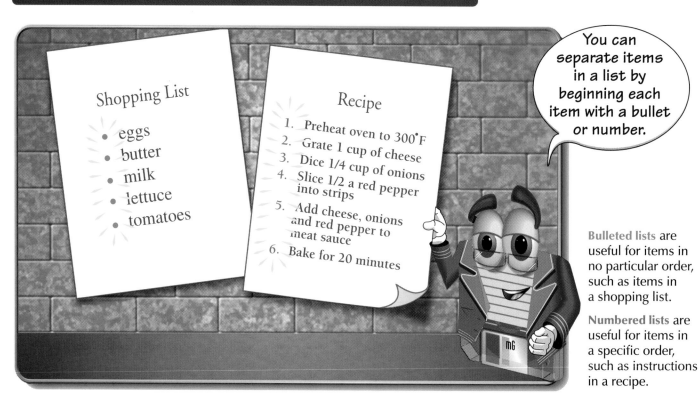

Shopping List
- eggs
- butter
- milk
- lettuce
- tomatoes

Recipe
1. Preheat oven to 300°F
2. Grate 1 cup of cheese
3. Dice 1/4 cup of onions
4. Slice 1/2 a red pepper into strips
5. Add cheese, onions and red pepper to meat sauce
6. Bake for 20 minutes

You can separate items in a list by beginning each item with a bullet or number.

Bulleted lists are useful for items in no particular order, such as items in a shopping list.

Numbered lists are useful for items in a specific order, such as instructions in a recipe.

CREATE A BULLETED OR NUMBERED LIST

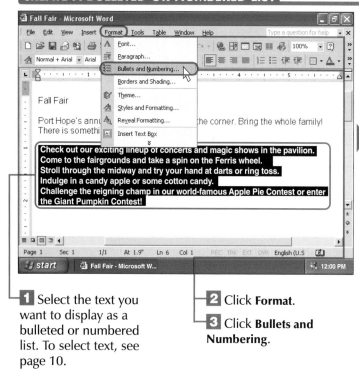

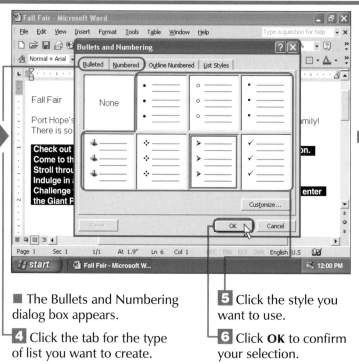

1 Select the text you want to display as a bulleted or numbered list. To select text, see page 10.

2 Click **Format**.

3 Click **Bullets and Numbering**.

■ The Bullets and Numbering dialog box appears.

4 Click the tab for the type of list you want to create.

5 Click the style you want to use.

6 Click **OK** to confirm your selection.

How can I create a bulleted or numbered list as I type?

1 Type * to create a bulleted list or type **1.** to create a numbered list. Then press the **Spacebar**.

2 Type the first item in the list and then press the **Enter** key. Word automatically adds a bullet or number for the next item.

3 Repeat step **2** for each item in the list.

4 To finish the list, press the **Enter** key twice.

Note: When you create a bulleted or numbered list as you type, the AutoCorrect Options button ( ) appears. You can click this button to specify that you do not want Word to create a bulleted or numbered list as you type.

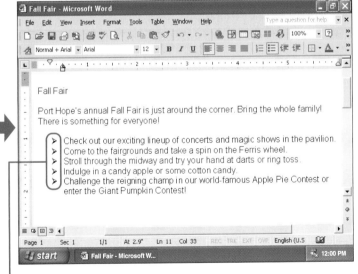

■ A bullet or number appears in front of each item in the list.

■ To deselect the text in the list, click outside the selected area.

■ To remove bullets or numbers from a list, repeat steps **1** to **6**, selecting **None** in step **5**.

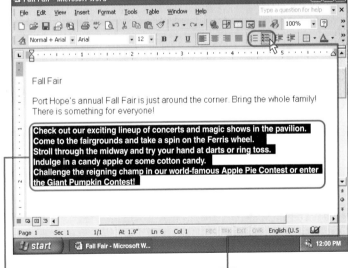

QUICKLY CREATE A LIST

1 Select the text you want to display as a bulleted or numbered list. To select text, see page 10.

2 Click one of the following buttons.

▤ Add numbers

▤ Add bullets

Note: If the button you want is not displayed, click ▸ on the Formatting toolbar to display the button.

INDENT PARAGRAPHS

You can indent text to make paragraphs in your document stand out.

INDENT PARAGRAPHS

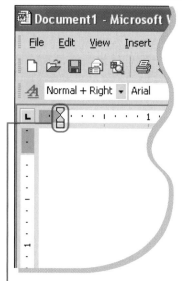

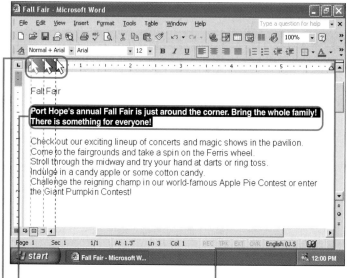

■ These symbols allow you to indent the left edge of a paragraph.

▽ Indent first line.
△ Indent all but the first line.
▢ Indent all lines.

■ This symbol (△) allows you to indent the right edge of a paragraph.

Note: If the ruler is not displayed, see page 38 to display the ruler.

1 Select the paragraph(s) you want to indent. To select text, see page 10.

2 Position the mouse ⃞ over the indent symbol you want to use to indent the text.

3 Drag the indent symbol to a new position on the ruler.

■ A dotted line shows the new indent position.

What types of indents can I create?

First Line Indent

Indents only the first line of a paragraph. First line indents are often used to mark the beginning of paragraphs in letters and professional documents.

Hanging Indent

Indents all but the first line of a paragraph. Hanging indents are useful when you are creating a glossary or bibliography.

Indent Both Sides

Indenting both the left and right sides of a paragraph is useful when you want to set text, such as a quotation, apart from the rest of the text in your document.

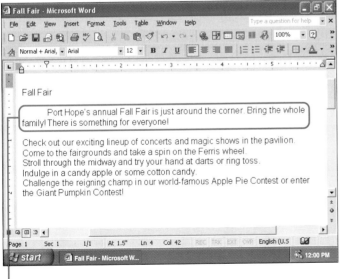

■ Word indents the paragraph(s) you selected.

■ To deselect text, click outside the selected area.

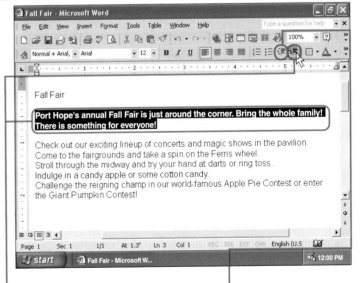

QUICKLY INDENT PARAGRAPHS

■1 Select the paragraph(s) you want to indent. To select text, see page 10.

■2 Click ⊞ to indent the left edge of the paragraph(s).

Note: If ⊞ is not displayed, click ┊ on the Formatting toolbar to display the button.

■ You can repeat step 2 to further indent the text.

■ To decrease the indent, click ⊞.

95

CHANGE TAB SETTINGS

You can use tabs to line up information in your document. Word offers several types of tabs for you to choose from.

Left Tab | Susan B. Thompson
President
ABC Toys Inc.

Derek Appleby Designs
1223 Lincoln Ave.
New York, N.Y. | Right Tab

Alice Spencer
207 Ocean View Drive
Miami, Florida
Center Tab

1156 | 93
42 | 67
835 | 02
Decimal Tab

Word automatically places a tab every 0.5 inches across a page.

CHANGE TAB SETTINGS

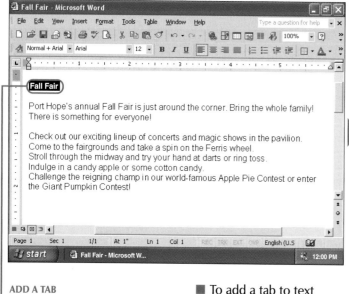

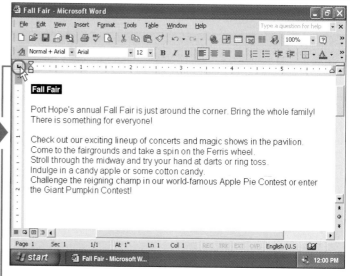

ADD A TAB

1 Select the text you want to use a new tab. To select text, see page 10.

■ To add a tab to text you are about to type, click the location in your document where you want to type the text.

2 Click this area until the type of tab you want to add appears.

   ⌊ Left tab

   ⊥ Center tab

   ⌋ Right tab

   ⊥ Decimal tab

Note: If the ruler is not displayed, see page 38 to display the ruler.

SIMPLIFY IT

How do I move a tab?

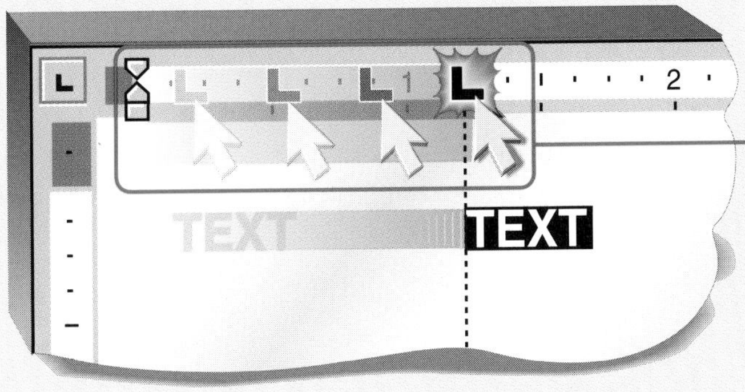

1 Select the text that uses the tab you want to move. To select text, see page 10.

2 Position the mouse over the tab you want to move and then drag the tab to a new location on the ruler. A dotted line shows the new location.

■ The text that uses the tab moves to the new location.

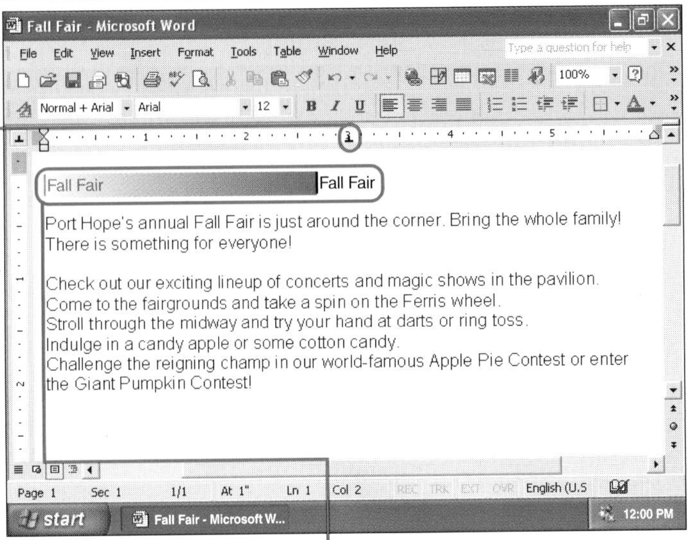

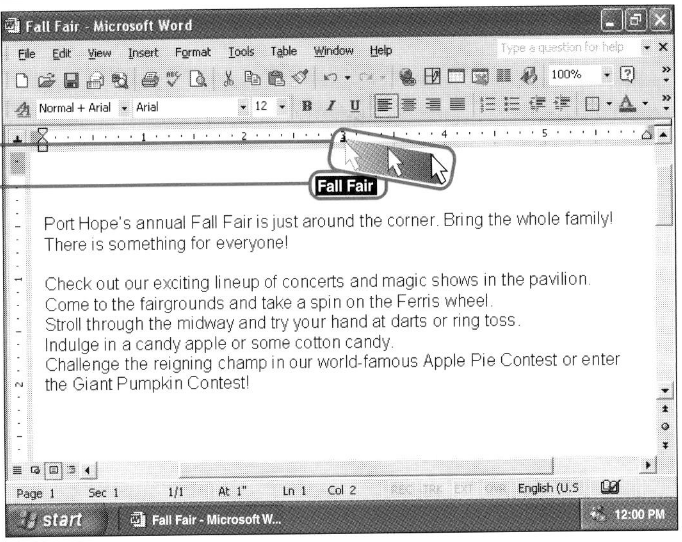

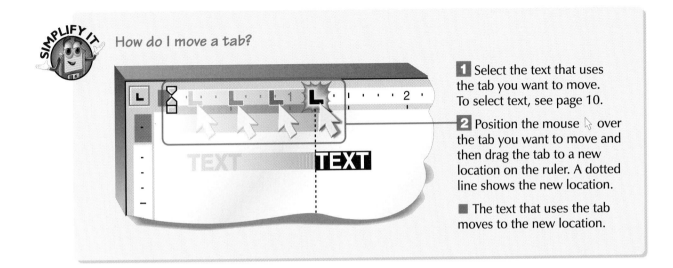

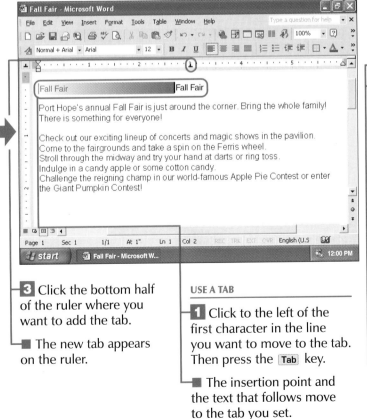

3 Click the bottom half of the ruler where you want to add the tab.

■ The new tab appears on the ruler.

USE A TAB

1 Click to the left of the first character in the line you want to move to the tab. Then press the Tab key.

■ The insertion point and the text that follows move to the tab you set.

REMOVE A TAB

1 Select the text that uses the tab you want to remove. To select text, see page 10.

2 Position the mouse over the tab you want to remove and then drag the tab downward off the ruler.

■ The tab disappears from the ruler.

■ To move the text back to the left margin, click to the left of the first character. Then press the Backspace key.

APPLY FORMATTING

Word keeps track of the formatting you have applied to text in your document. You can apply the formatting to another area of text.

APPLY FORMATTING TO ONE AREA OF TEXT

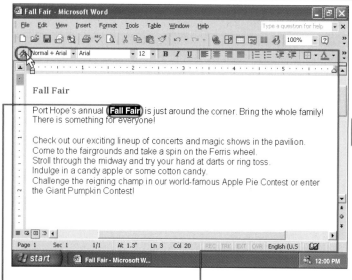

1 Select the text you want to apply formatting to. To select text, see page 10.

2 Click 🖺 to display the Styles and Formatting task pane.

Note: If 🖺 is not displayed, click ⟩⟩ on the Formatting toolbar to display the button.

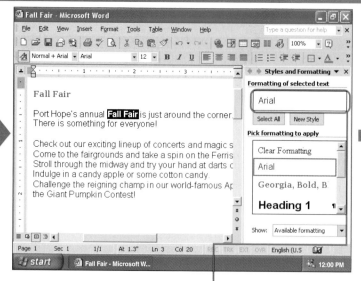

■ The Styles and Formatting task pane appears.

■ This area describes the current formatting of the text you selected.

Is there another way to apply formatting to text in my document?

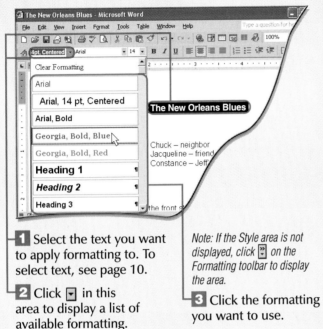

1 Select the text you want to apply formatting to. To select text, see page 10.

2 Click ▼ in this area to display a list of available formatting.

Note: If the Style area is not displayed, click ⮟ on the Formatting toolbar to display the area.

3 Click the formatting you want to use.

Can I remove formatting I have applied to text?

You can remove formatting you have applied to text in your document. Perform steps **1** to **3** below, selecting **Clear Formatting** in step **3**.

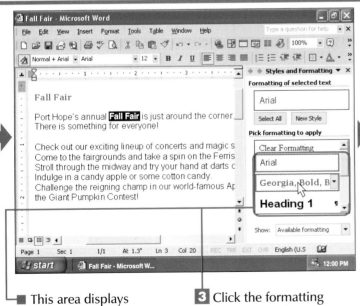

■ This area displays formatting you have used in your document.

Note: The area also displays formatting included with Word.

3 Click the formatting you want to apply to the text.

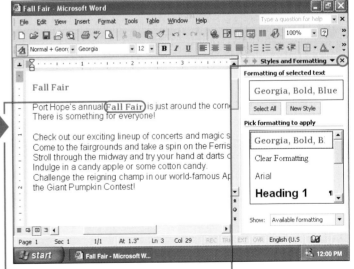

■ The text you selected displays the new formatting.

■ To deselect text, click outside the selected area.

■ To hide the Styles and Formatting task pane, click ✕ .

CONTINUED

99

APPLY FORMATTING

Impact, 18 pt, Regular, Blue

> You can instantly change the appearance of all the text in a document that displays the same formatting. This saves you time and keeps the appearance of text in your document consistent.

APPLY FORMATTING TO MANY AREAS OF TEXT

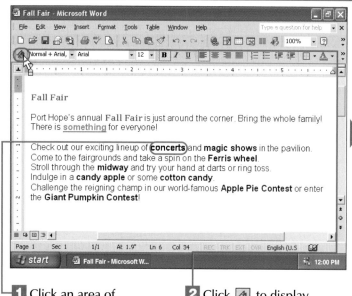

1 Click an area of text that displays the formatting you want to change throughout your document.

2 Click 🖳 to display the Styles and Formatting task pane.

Note: If 🖳 is not displayed, click ⟩⟩ on the Formatting toolbar to display the button.

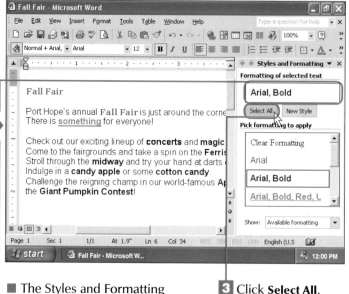

■ The Styles and Formatting task pane appears.

■ This area describes the current formatting of the text you selected.

3 Click **Select All**.

SIMPLIFY IT

The Styles and Formatting task pane does not display the formatting I want to apply. What can I do?

Perform steps 1 to 3 below to select the areas of text you want to format. You can then format the text as you would format any text in a document. For example, you can change the font, size, color or alignment of the text. To format text, see pages 78 to 87.

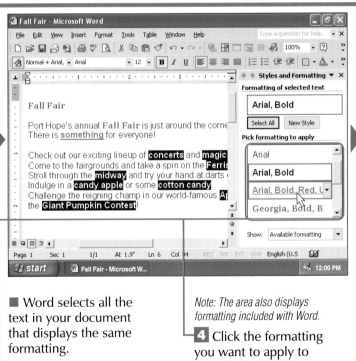

■ Word selects all the text in your document that displays the same formatting.

■ This area displays formatting you have used in your document.

Note: The area also displays formatting included with Word.

4 Click the formatting you want to apply to the selected text.

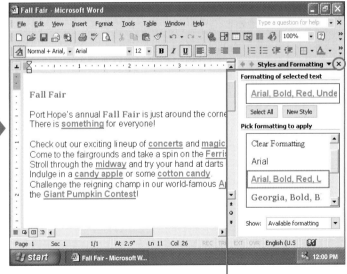

■ The selected text displays the new formatting.

■ To deselect text, click outside a selected area.

■ To hide the Styles and Formatting task pane, click ⊠.

REVIEW FORMATTING

Plot Summary
ACT I

Scene I

Tim and Jeff are sitting on the front steps of their house on a side street in New Orleans. Tim is trying to convince his son to let go of his dream of becoming a famous jazz saxophonist. Upset with his father for meddling in his life, Jeff storms

REVIEW FORMATTING

Font:
 Arial
 10 pt
 Bold
 Font color: Red
Language:
 English

> You can review details about the formatting applied to text in a document. This is useful when you want to determine exactly what formatting was applied to the text.

REVIEW FORMATTING

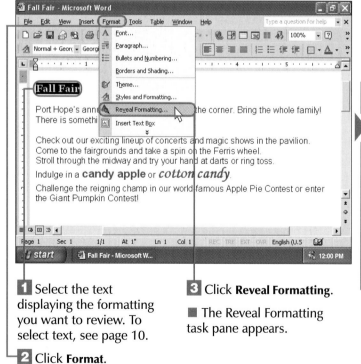

1 Select the text displaying the formatting you want to review. To select text, see page 10.

2 Click **Format**.

3 Click **Reveal Formatting**.

■ The Reveal Formatting task pane appears.

■ This area displays a sample of the text you selected.

■ This area displays the formatting details for the text.

4 To change the formatting of the text you selected, click the blue, underlined heading for the type of formatting you want to change.

SIMPLIFY IT

What types of formatting can I review using the Reveal Formatting task pane?

The Reveal Formatting task pane allows you to review several types of formatting including font, paragraph and section formatting. For example, you can review paragraph formatting to determine the alignment of the paragraph or review section formatting to determine the margin settings for the section.

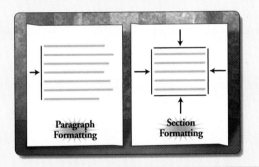

Paragraph Formatting   Section Formatting

SIMPLIFY IT

When reviewing formatting, how can I display more details?

Each item that displays a plus sign (⊞) contains hidden details. To display the hidden details, click the plus sign (⊞) beside the item (⊞ changes to ⊟). To once again hide the details, click the minus sign (⊟) beside the item.

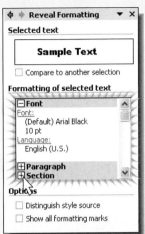

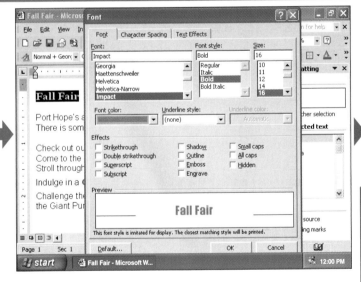

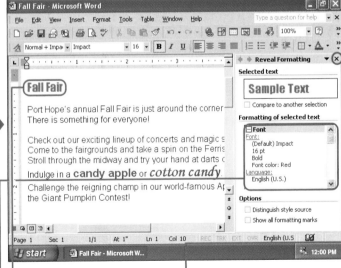

■ In this example, the Font dialog box appears.

Note: The dialog box that appears depends on the blue, underlined heading you selected.

5 Perform steps **5** to **11** starting on page 86 to change the font.

■ The text you selected displays the formatting changes.

■ This area displays the new formatting details.

■ To deselect text, click outside the selected area.

■ To hide the Reveal Formatting task pane, click ✕.

CONTINUED

103

REVIEW FORMATTING

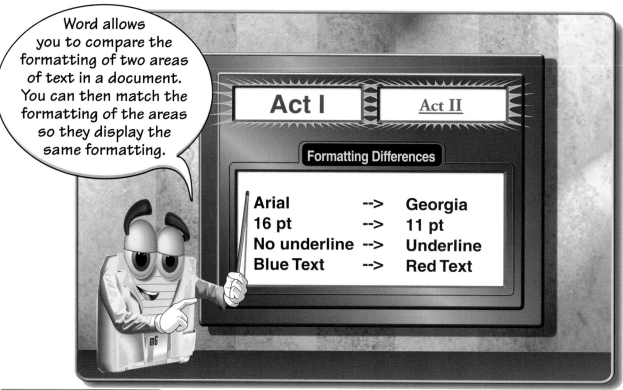

Word allows you to compare the formatting of two areas of text in a document. You can then match the formatting of the areas so they display the same formatting.

COMPARE FORMATTING

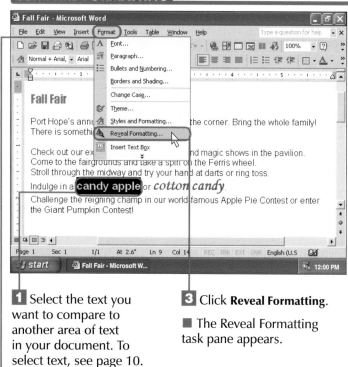

1 Select the text you want to compare to another area of text in your document. To select text, see page 10.

2 Click **Format**.

3 Click **Reveal Formatting**.

■ The Reveal Formatting task pane appears.

4 Click **Compare to another selection** (☐ changes to ☑).

5 Select the text you want to compare to the text you selected in step 1.

■ This area displays samples of the two areas of text you selected.

■ This area indicates the formatting differences between the two areas of text.

Note: If there are no differences, the area displays the text **No formatting differences**.

When would I need to compare formatting?

You should compare formatting in a document that may contain inconsistent formatting. For example, when formatting a long document, you may have applied different formatting to different areas of the document. If you created a new document by copying text from other documents, the new document may display several different types of formatting.

How can I ensure the formatting in my documents is consistent?

You can use the Styles and Formatting task pane to apply consistent formatting to text in your documents. For information on using the Styles and Formatting task pane, see pages 98 to 101.

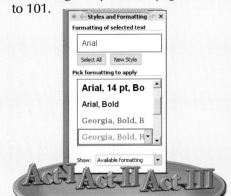

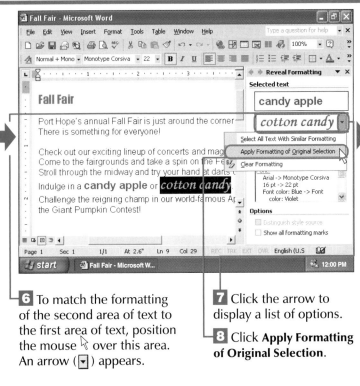

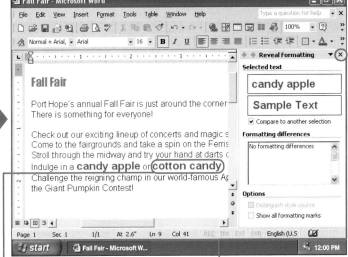

6 To match the formatting of the second area of text to the first area of text, position the mouse ⌖ over this area. An arrow (▼) appears.

7 Click the arrow to display a list of options.

8 Click **Apply Formatting of Original Selection**.

■ Word changes the formatting of the second area of text to match the formatting of the first area of text.

■ To deselect text, click outside the selected area.

■ To hide the Reveal Formatting task pane, click ✕.

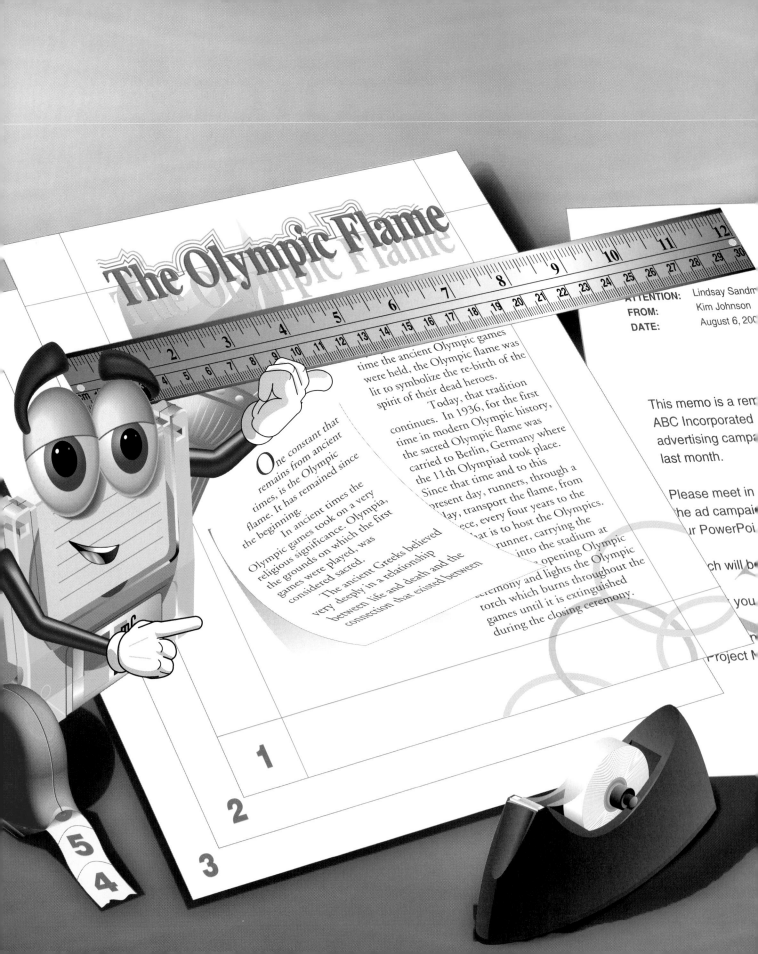

CHAPTER 6

FORMAT PAGES

Are you wondering how to change the appearance of pages in your document? In this chapter, you will learn how to add page numbers, change margins, create newspaper columns and more.

INSERT A PAGE BREAK

You can insert a page break to start a new page at a specific location in your document. A page break indicates where one page ends and another begins.

Inserting a page break is useful when you want a heading to appear at the top of a new page.

INSERT A PAGE BREAK

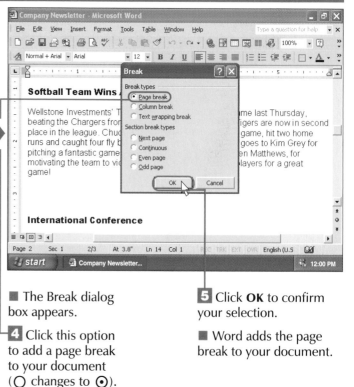

1 Click the location in your document where you want to start a new page.

2 Click **Insert**.

3 Click **Break**.

■ The Break dialog box appears.

4 Click this option to add a page break to your document (○ changes to ◉).

5 Click **OK** to confirm your selection.

■ Word adds the page break to your document.

Will Word ever insert a page break automatically?

When you fill a page with information, Word automatically inserts a page break to start a new page.

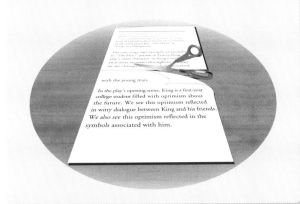

How can I quickly insert a page break?

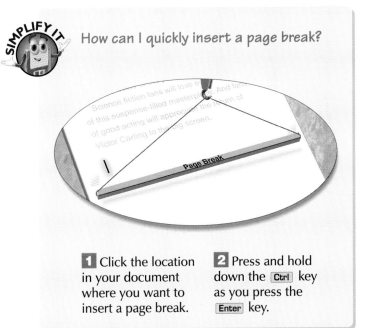

1 Click the location in your document where you want to insert a page break.

2 Press and hold down the `Ctrl` key as you press the `Enter` key.

DELETE A PAGE BREAK

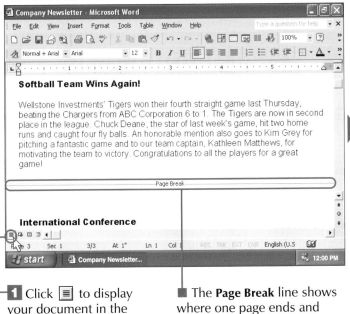

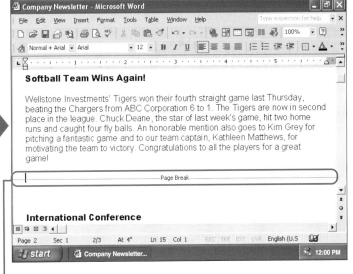

1 Click ▤ to display your document in the Normal view.

■ The **Page Break** line shows where one page ends and another begins. The line will not appear when you print your document.

Note: You may need to scroll through your document to view the line.

2 Click the **Page Break** line.

3 Press the `Delete` key to remove the page break.

INSERT A SECTION BREAK

You can insert section breaks to divide your document into sections.

Dividing your document into sections allows you to apply different formatting to each section. For example, you may want to add newspaper columns or change the margins for only part of your document.

INSERT A SECTION BREAK

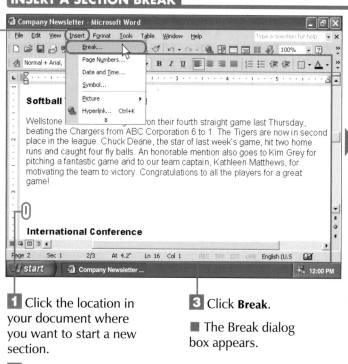

1 Click the location in your document where you want to start a new section.

2 Click **Insert**.

3 Click **Break**.

■ The Break dialog box appears.

4 Click the type of section break you want to add (○ changes to ⊙).

Next page - Starts a new section on a new page.

Continuous - Starts a new section on the current page.

5 Click **OK** to confirm your selection.

■ Word adds the section break to your document.

Will the appearance of my document change when I delete a section break?

When you delete a section break, the text above the break assumes the appearance of the text below the break. For example, if the text below a section break appears in newspaper columns, the text above the break will also appear in newspaper columns when you delete the break.

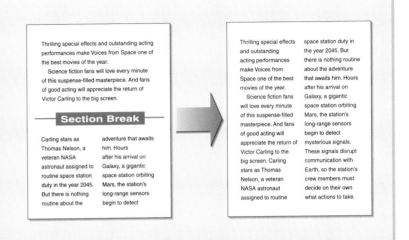

DELETE A SECTION BREAK

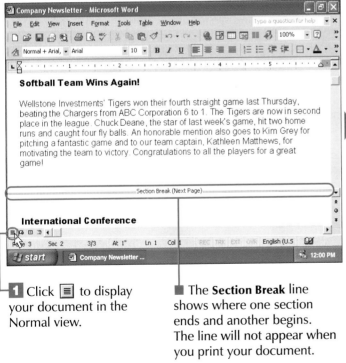

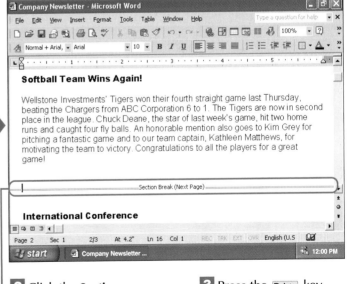

1 Click ≡ to display your document in the Normal view.

■ The **Section Break** line shows where one section ends and another begins. The line will not appear when you print your document.

Note: You may need to scroll through your document to view the line.

2 Click the **Section Break** line.

3 Press the Delete key to remove the section break.

ADD PAGE NUMBERS

You can have Word number the pages in your document.

Word can display page numbers only in the Print Layout view. To change the view of a document, see page 36.

ADD PAGE NUMBERS

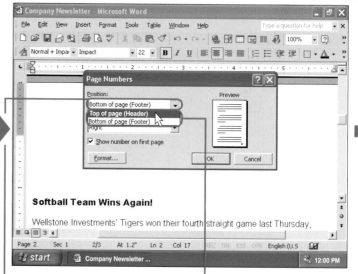

1 Click **Insert**.

2 Click **Page Numbers**.

■ The Page Numbers dialog box appears.

3 Click this area to select a position for the page numbers.

4 Click the position where you want the page numbers to appear.

How do I remove page numbers from my document?

Deleting a page number from your document's header or footer will remove all the page numbers from your document.

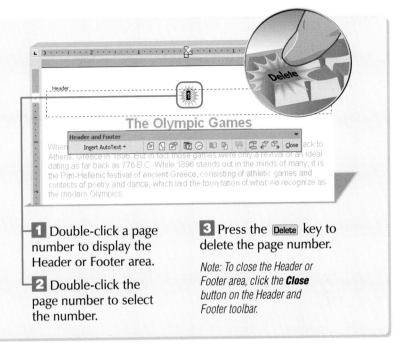

1 Double-click a page number to display the Header or Footer area.

2 Double-click the page number to select the number.

3 Press the Delete key to delete the page number.

Note: To close the Header or Footer area, click the **Close** button on the Header and Footer toolbar.

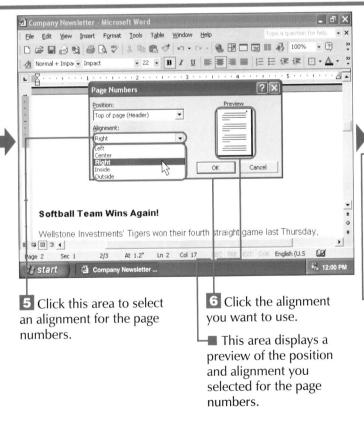

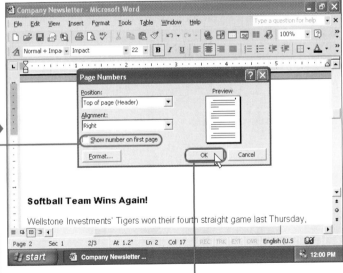

5 Click this area to select an alignment for the page numbers.

6 Click the alignment you want to use.

■ This area displays a preview of the position and alignment you selected for the page numbers.

7 If you want to hide the page number on the first page of your document, click this option (☑ changes to ☐).

Note: Turning off this option is useful if the first page in your document is a title page.

8 Click **OK** to add the page numbers to your document.

■ If you later make changes that affect the pages in your document, such as adding or removing text, Word will automatically adjust the page numbers for you.

ADD A HEADER OR FOOTER

You can add a header or footer to display additional information on each page of your document. A header or footer can contain information such as a chapter title, a page number or the current date.

A **header** appears at the top of each printed page.

A **footer** appears at the bottom of each printed page.

Word can display headers and footers only in the Print Layout view. To change the view of a document, see page 36.

ADD A HEADER OR FOOTER

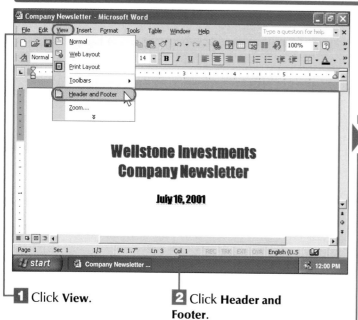

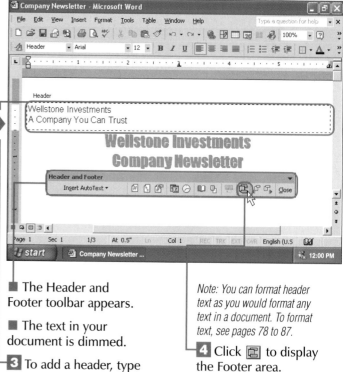

1 Click **View**.

2 Click **Header and Footer**.

■ The Header and Footer toolbar appears.

■ The text in your document is dimmed.

3 To add a header, type the header text.

Note: You can format header text as you would format any text in a document. To format text, see pages 78 to 87.

4 Click 📄 to display the Footer area.

Can I edit a header or footer?

Yes. Double-click the dimmed text for the header or footer you want to edit. You can then edit the header or footer text as you would edit any text in a document. To edit text, see page 46. When you finish editing header or footer text, perform step 6 below.

How do I remove a header or footer from my document?

Double-click the dimmed text for the header or footer you want to remove. Drag the mouse I over the header or footer text until you highlight all the text. Then press the Delete key to remove the header or footer from your document. When you finish deleting header or footer text, perform step 6 below.

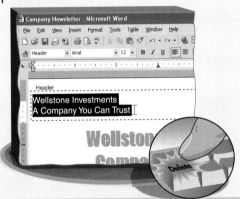

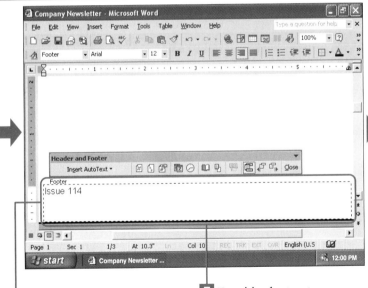

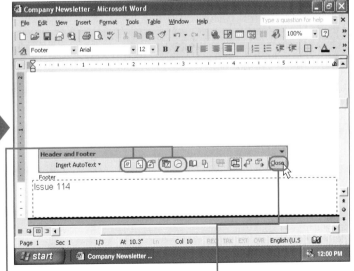

■ The Footer area appears.

Note: You can repeat step 4 to return to the Header area at any time.

5 To add a footer, type the footer text.

Note: You can format footer text as you would format any text in a document. To format text, see pages 78 to 87.

■ You can click one of the following buttons to quickly insert information into a header or footer.

#️ Page number
#️ Total number of pages
📅 Date
🕐 Time

6 When you finish adding the header and footer to your document, click **Close**.

ADD FOOTNOTES OR ENDNOTES

You can add a footnote or endnote to provide additional information about text in your document. Footnotes and endnotes can provide information such as an explanation, comment or reference.

Word displays footnotes and endnotes as they will appear on a printed page in the Print Layout view. For information on the views, see page 36.

ADD FOOTNOTES OR ENDNOTES

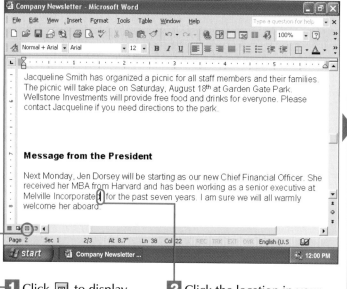

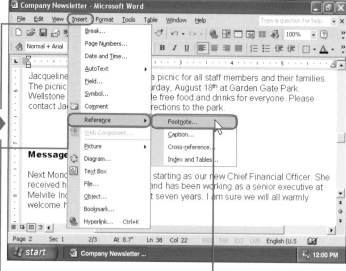

1 Click 🔲 to display your document in the Print Layout view.

2 Click the location in your document where you want the number for the footnote or endnote to appear.

Note: The footnote or endnote number will appear where the insertion point flashes on your screen.

3 Click **Insert**.

4 Click **Reference**.

Note: If Reference does not appear on the menu, position the mouse ⌖ over the bottom of the menu to display all the menu options.

5 Click **Footnote**.

What is the difference between footnotes and endnotes?

Footnotes

By default, footnotes appear at the bottom of a page. Word ensures that the text for a footnote appears on the same page as the footnote number.

Endnotes

By default, endnotes appear at the end of a document.

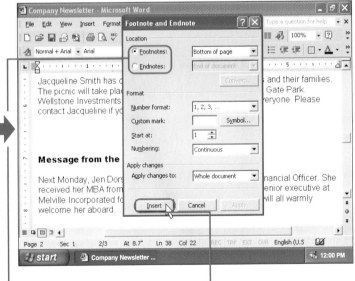

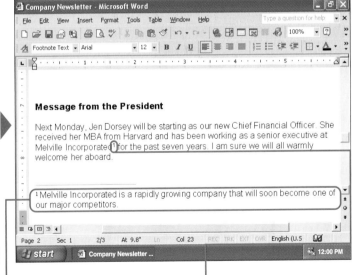

■ The Footnote and Endnote dialog box appears.

6 Click **Footnotes** or **Endnotes** to specify the type of note you want to add (○ changes to ⊙).

7 Click **Insert** to add the note to your document.

■ Word displays the footnote or endnote area.

8 Type the text for the footnote or endnote. You can format the text as you would format any text in a document. To format text, see pages 78 to 87.

■ The number for the footnote or endnote appears in your document.

Note: You may need to scroll through your document to view the number.

CONTINUED ►

You can view and edit a footnote or endnote you added to your document. You can also delete a footnote or endnote you no longer need.

VIEW FOOTNOTES OR ENDNOTES

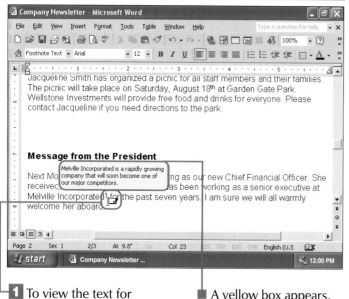

1 To view the text for a footnote or endnote, position the mouse I over the footnote or endnote number in your document (I changes to 🔲).

■ A yellow box appears, displaying the text for the footnote or endnote.

EDIT FOOTNOTES OR ENDNOTES

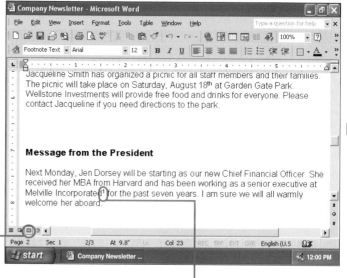

1 Click 🔲 to display your document in the Print Layout view.

2 To edit the text for a footnote or endnote, double-click the footnote or endnote number in your document.

How can I print endnotes on a separate page?

Word automatically prints endnotes after the last line in your document. To print endnotes on a separate page, you need to insert a page break directly above the endnote area. To insert a page break, see page 108.

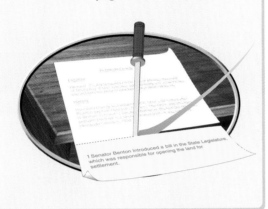

Can I copy a footnote or endnote?

Yes. Copying a footnote or endnote is useful when you want to provide the same comment or reference for several areas of text.

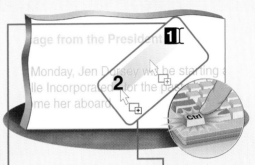

1 To copy a note, drag the mouse I over the footnote or endnote number until you highlight the number.

2 Press and hold down the Ctrl key as you drag the number to a new location.

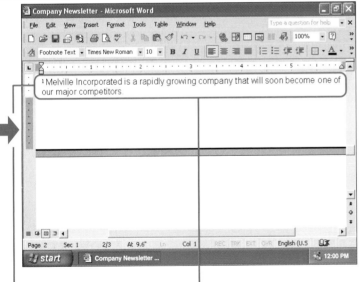

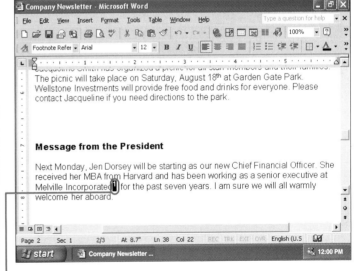

■ The corresponding footnote or endnote area appears.

■ You can edit the text for a footnote or endnote as you would edit any text in a document. To edit text, see page 46.

DELETE FOOTNOTES OR ENDNOTES

1 Drag the mouse I over the number for the footnote or endnote you want to delete until you highlight the number.

2 Press the Delete key.

■ The footnote or endnote disappears from your document.

■ Word automatically renumbers the remaining footnotes or endnotes in your document.

You can change the margins in your document to suit your needs. A margin is the space between the text in your document and the edge of your paper.

Word automatically sets the top and bottom margins to 1 inch and the left and right margins to 1.25 inches.

Changing the margins allows you to fit more or less information on a page and can help you accommodate letterhead and other specialty paper.

CHANGE MARGINS

1 Click anywhere in the document or section where you want to change the margins.

Note: To change the margins for only part of your document, you must divide the document into sections. To divide a document into sections, see page 110.

2 Click **File**.

3 Click **Page Setup**.

■ The Page Setup dialog box appears.

Is there another way to change the margins for my document?

Yes. In the Print Layout view, margins are shown in gray on the ruler. To change a margin, position the mouse ↗ over the edge of the margin (↗ changes to ↔ or ↕) and then drag the margin to a new location on the ruler.

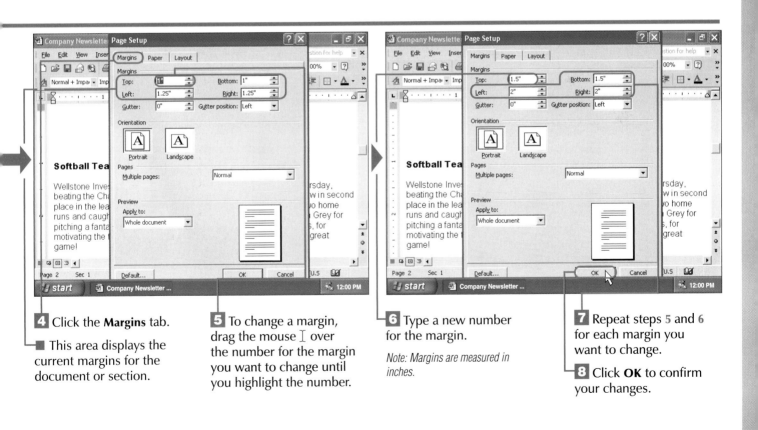

4 Click the **Margins** tab.

■ This area displays the current margins for the document or section.

5 To change a margin, drag the mouse I over the number for the margin you want to change until you highlight the number.

6 Type a new number for the margin.

Note: Margins are measured in inches.

7 Repeat steps **5** and **6** for each margin you want to change.

8 Click **OK** to confirm your changes.

You can vertically center the text on each page in your document. Vertically centering text is useful when creating title pages and short memos.

When you vertically center text on a page, Word centers the text between the top and bottom margins of the page. For information on margins, see page 120.

Word can display text vertically centered on a page only in the Print Layout view. To change the view of a document, see page 36.

CENTER TEXT ON A PAGE

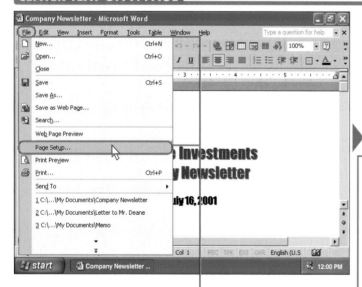

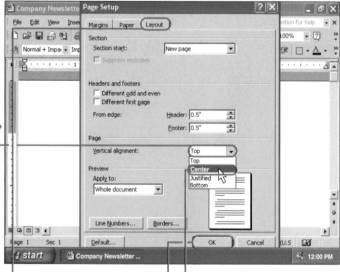

1 Click anywhere in the document or section you want to vertically center.

Note: To vertically center only part of your document, you must divide the document into sections. To divide a document into sections, see page 110.

2 Click **File**.

3 Click **Page Setup**.

■ The Page Setup dialog box appears.

4 Click the **Layout** tab.

5 Click this area to display the vertical alignment options.

6 Click **Center** to vertically center the text.

7 Click **OK** to confirm your change.

■ To remove the centering, repeat steps **1** to **7**, selecting **Top** in step **6**.

CHANGE PAGE ORIENTATION

You can change the orientation of pages in your document. The page orientation determines the direction information prints on a page.

Portrait

Portrait is the standard page orientation and is used to print most documents, such as letters, memos and reports.

Landscape

Landscape prints information across the long side of a page and is often used to print certificates and tables.

CHANGE PAGE ORIENTATION

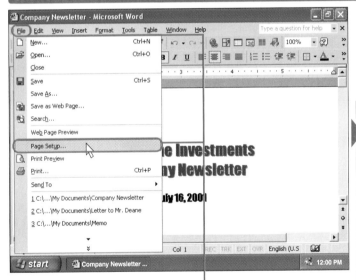

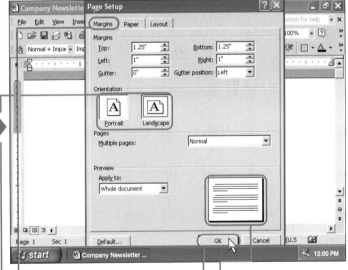

1 Click anywhere in the document or section you want to change to a different page orientation.

Note: To change the page orientation for only part of your document, you must divide the document into sections. To divide a document into sections, see page 110.

2 Click **File**.

3 Click **Page Setup**.

■ The Page Setup dialog box appears.

4 Click the **Margins** tab.

5 Click the page orientation you want to use.

■ This area displays a preview of how your document will appear.

6 Click **OK** to confirm your change.

ADD A WATERMARK

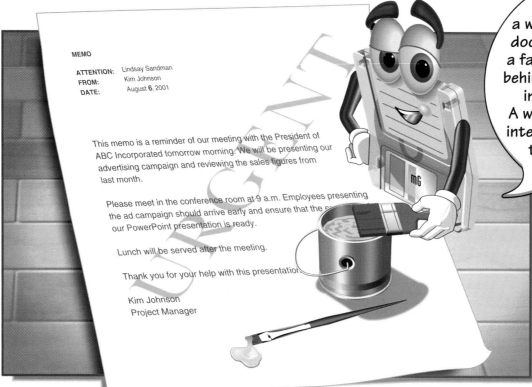

> You can add a watermark to your document to display a faint picture or text behind the information in the document. A watermark can add interest to or identify the status of a document.

Word can display watermarks only in the Print Layout view. To change the view of a document, see page 36.

ADD A WATERMARK

1 Click **Format**.

2 Click **Background**.

Note: If Background does not appear on the menu, position the mouse ☐ over the bottom of the menu to display all the menu options.

3 Click **Printed Watermark**.

■ The Printed Watermark dialog box appears.

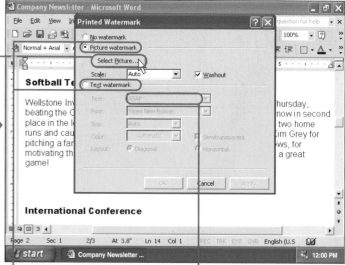

4 Click an option to specify the type of watermark you want to add (○ changes to ◉).

5 If you selected **Picture watermark** in step 4, click **Select Picture** to locate the picture you want to use.

■ If you selected **Text watermark** in step 4, double-click the text in this area and then type the text you want to use. Then skip to step 8.

124

Does Word provide any text watermarks that I can use?

Yes. Word provides several text watermarks including ASAP, CONFIDENTIAL, PERSONAL and URGENT, that you can add to your document.

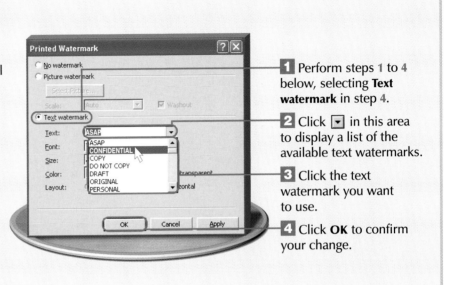

1 Perform steps **1** to **4** below, selecting **Text watermark** in step **4**.

2 Click ▼ in this area to display a list of the available text watermarks.

3 Click the text watermark you want to use.

4 Click **OK** to confirm your change.

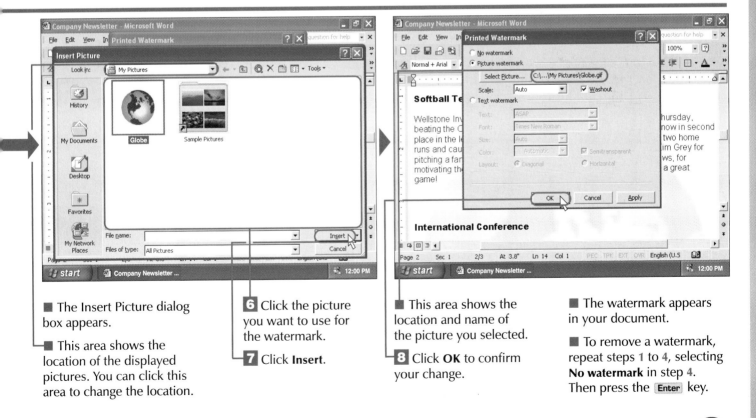

■ The Insert Picture dialog box appears.

■ This area shows the location of the displayed pictures. You can click this area to change the location.

6 Click the picture you want to use for the watermark.

7 Click **Insert**.

■ This area shows the location and name of the picture you selected.

8 Click **OK** to confirm your change.

■ The watermark appears in your document.

■ To remove a watermark, repeat steps **1** to **4**, selecting **No watermark** in step **4**. Then press the Enter key.

You can place a border around each page of your document to enhance the appearance of the document.

Word can display page borders only in the Print Layout view. To change the view of a document, see page 36.

Line Borders

You can use a line border for certificates and title pages.

Art Borders

You can use a colorful art border to enhance invitations and newsletters.

ADD A PAGE BORDER

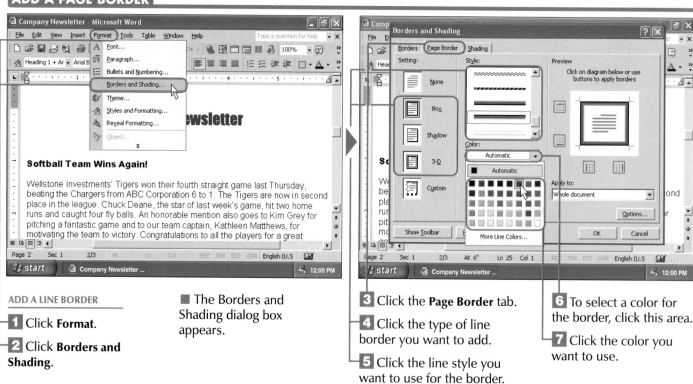

ADD A LINE BORDER

1 Click **Format**.

2 Click **Borders and Shading**.

■ The Borders and Shading dialog box appears.

3 Click the **Page Border** tab.

4 Click the type of line border you want to add.

5 Click the line style you want to use for the border.

6 To select a color for the border, click this area.

7 Click the color you want to use.

Why does a dialog box appear when I try to add an art border to my document?

A dialog box appears if the art borders are not installed on your computer. Insert the CD-ROM disc you used to install Word into your computer's CD-ROM drive. Then click **Yes** to install the art borders.

Note: A window may appear on your screen. Click ☒ *in the top right corner of the window to close the window.*

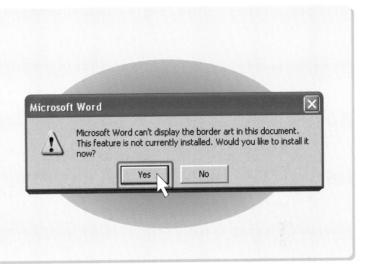

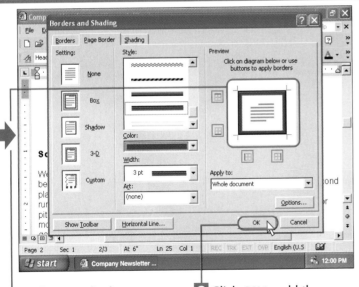

■ This area displays a preview of the border you selected.

8 Click **OK** to add the border to your document.

■ To remove a line border, repeat steps **1** to **4**, selecting **None** in step **4**. Then perform step **8**.

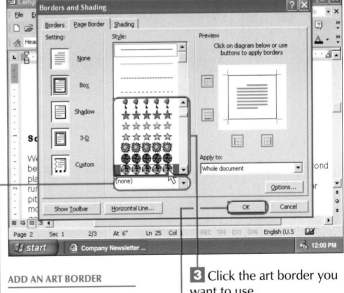

ADD AN ART BORDER

1 Perform steps **1** to **3** on page 126.

2 Click this area to display the available art borders.

Note: If a dialog box appears, see the top of this page.

3 Click the art border you want to use.

4 Click **OK**.

■ To remove an art border, perform steps **1** to **4** on page 126, selecting **None** in step **4**. Then perform step **8**.

CREATE NEWSPAPER COLUMNS

You can display text in columns like those found in a newspaper. Creating columns is useful in documents such as newsletters and brochures.

CREATE NEWSPAPER COLUMNS

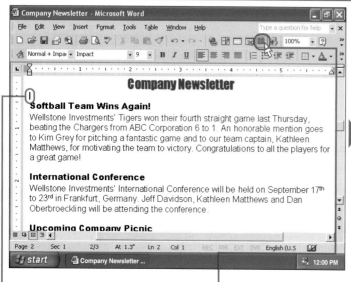

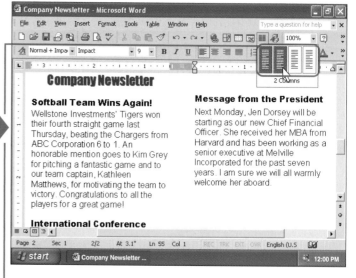

1 Click anywhere in the document or section you want to display in newspaper columns.

Note: To create newspaper columns for only part of your document, you must divide the document into sections. To divide a document into sections, see page 110.

2 Click ▦ to create newspaper columns.

Note: If ▦ is not displayed, click ⁑ on the Standard toolbar to display the button.

3 Drag the mouse ▷ until you highlight the number of columns you want to create.

■ The text in the document or section appears in newspaper columns.

■ Word will fill one column with text before starting a new column.

■ To remove newspaper columns, repeat steps **1** to **3**, selecting one column in step **3**.

128

Why do the newspaper columns disappear when I change the view of my document?

Word can display newspaper columns side by side only in the Print Layout view. To change the view of a document, see page 36.

How do I remove a column break?

If you want to move text back to the previous column, you can remove a column break.

Softball Team Wins Again!
Wellstone Investments' Tigers won their fourth straight game last Thursday, beating the Chargers from ABC Corporation 6 to 1. An honorable mention goes to Kim Grey for pitching a fantastic game and to our team captain, Kathleen Matthews, for motivating the team to victory. Congratulations to all the players for a great game!

········Column Break········

International Conference
Wellstone Investments' International

1 Click ▤ to display your document in the Normal view.

2 Click the **Column Break** line.

3 Press the Delete key to remove the column break.

INSERT A COLUMN BREAK

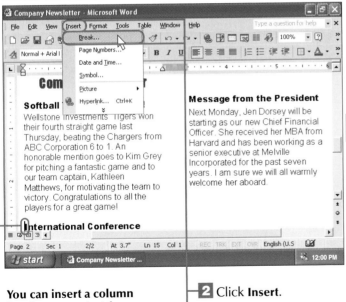

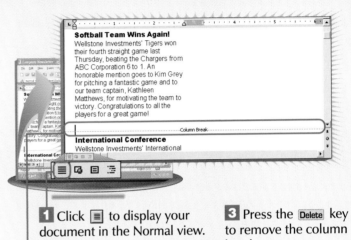

You can insert a column break to move text from one column to the top of the next column.

1 Click to the left of the text you want to move to the next column.

2 Click **Insert**.

3 Click **Break**.

■ The Break dialog box appears.

4 Click this option to add a column break (○ changes to ◉).

5 Click **OK** to confirm your selection.

■ Word moves the text after the insertion point to the top of the next column.

129

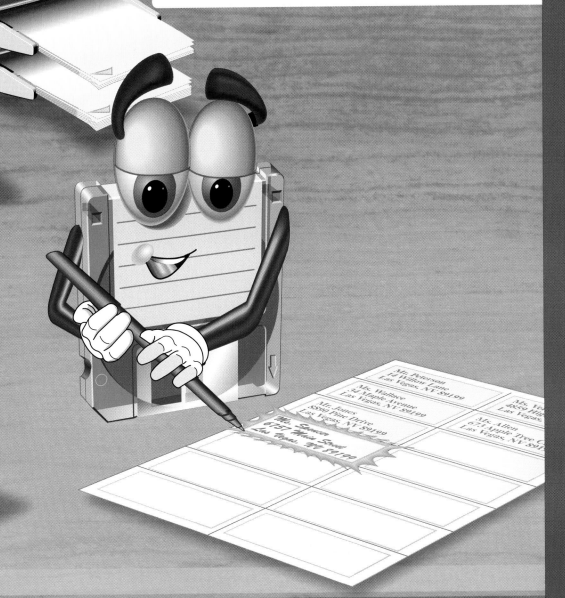

CHAPTER 7

PRINT DOCUMENTS

Are you ready to print your document? In this chapter, you will learn how to print documents, envelopes and labels.

You can use the Print Preview feature to see how your document will look when printed.

This allows you to confirm that the document will print the way you expect.

PREVIEW A DOCUMENT BEFORE PRINTING

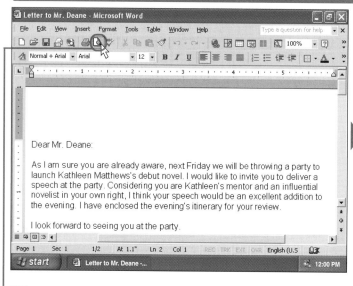

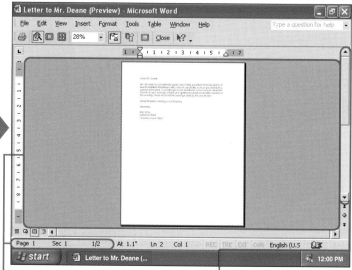

1 Click 🔍 to preview your document before printing.

Note: If 🔍 is not displayed, click 🔽 on the Standard toolbar to display the button.

■ The Print Preview window appears.

■ This area displays a page from your document.

■ This area indicates which page is displayed and the total number of pages in your document.

■ If your document contains more than one page, you can use the scroll bar to view the other pages.

SIMPLIFY IT

Can I edit my document in the Print Preview window?

Yes. If the mouse pointer looks like I when over your document, you can edit the document. If the mouse pointer looks like ⊕ or ⊖ when over your document, you can enlarge or reduce the size of the page displayed on your screen. To change the appearance of the mouse pointer, click the Magnifier button (🔍).

SIMPLIFY IT

Can I shrink the text in my document to fit on one less page?

If the last page in your document contains only a few lines of text, Word can shrink the text in your document to fit on one less page. In the Print Preview window, click the Shrink to Fit button (📑) to shrink the text in your document.

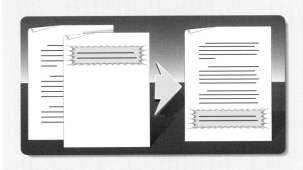

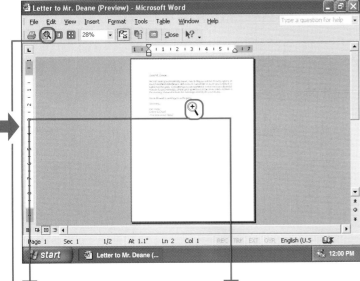

2 To magnify an area of the page, position the mouse ⬡ over the area you want to magnify (⬡ changes to ⊕).

■ If the mouse pointer looks like I when over the page, click 🔍.

3 Click the area to magnify the area.

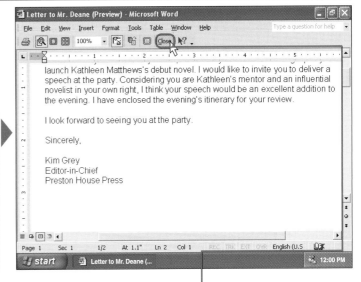

■ A magnified view of the area appears.

4 To once again display the entire page, click anywhere on the page.

5 When you finish previewing your document, click **Close** to close the Print Preview window.

You can produce a paper copy of the document displayed on your screen.

Before printing a document, make sure your printer is turned on and contains paper.

PRINT A DOCUMENT

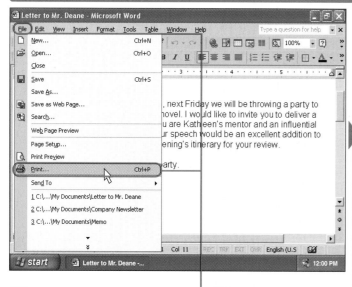

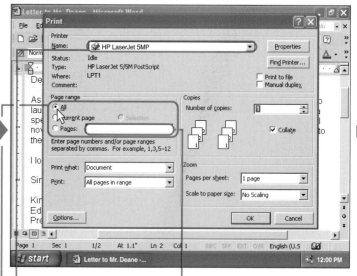

1 Click anywhere in the document or page you want to print.

■ To print only some of the text in the document, select the text you want to print. To select text, see page 10.

2 Click **File**.

3 Click **Print**.

■ The Print dialog box appears.

■ This area displays the printer that will print your document. You can click this area to select a different printer.

4 Click the print option you want to use (○ changes to ⊙).

Note: For information on the print options, see the top of page 135.

■ If you selected **Pages** in step 4, type the pages you want to print in this area (example: 1,3,5 or 2-4).

SIMPLIFY IT

Which print option should I use?

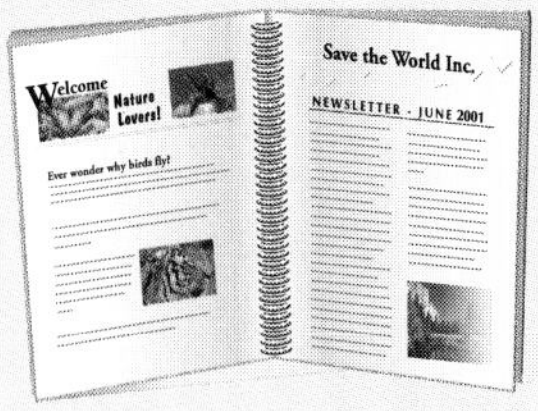

All

Prints every page in the document.

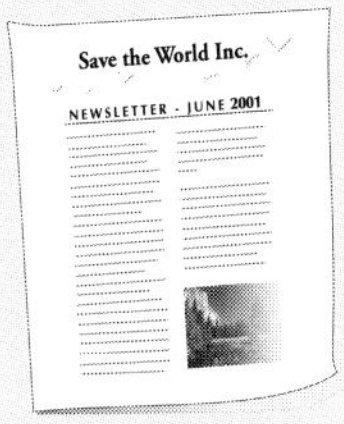

Current page

Prints the page containing the insertion point.

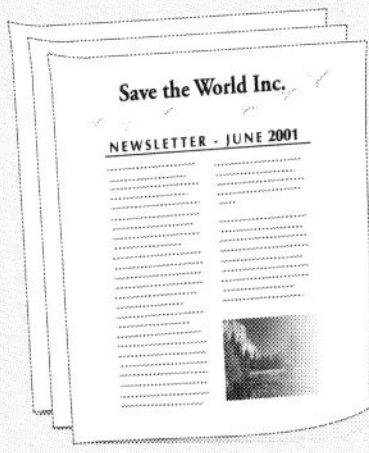

Pages

Prints the pages you specify.

Selection

Prints the text you selected.

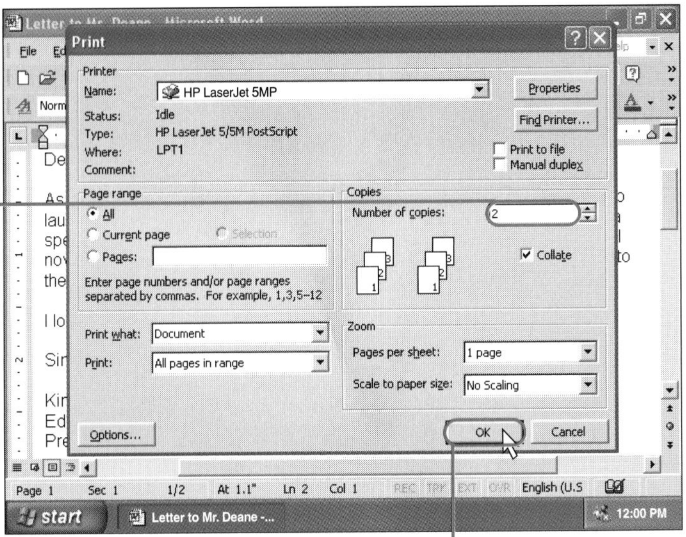

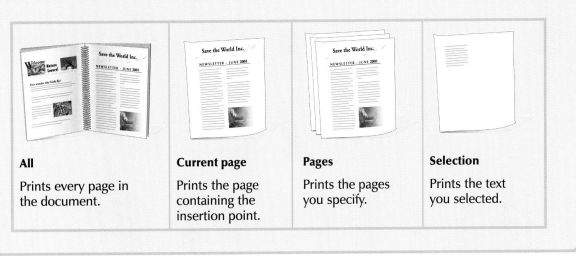

5 To print more than one copy of the document, double-click the number in this area and then type the number of copies you want to print.

6 Click **OK**.

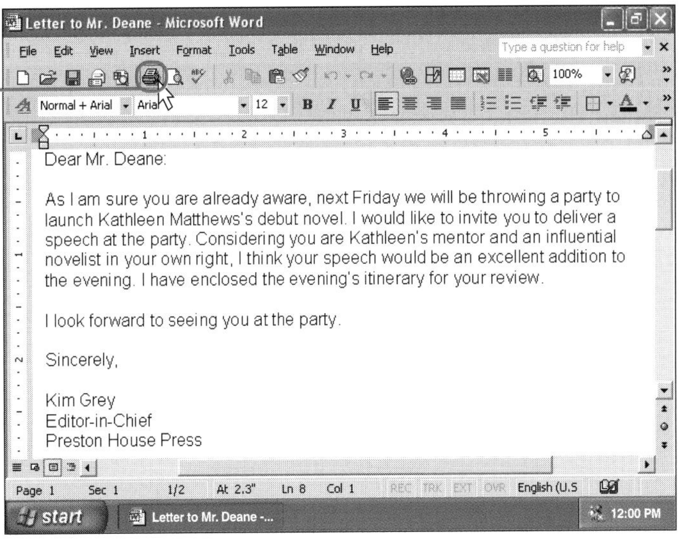

QUICKLY PRINT ENTIRE DOCUMENT

1 Click [print icon] to quickly print your entire document.

Note: If [print icon] is not displayed, click [»] on the Standard toolbar to display the button.

Before you begin, make sure your printer can print envelopes. You can consult the manual that came with your printer to determine if your printer can print envelopes.

PRINT AN ENVELOPE

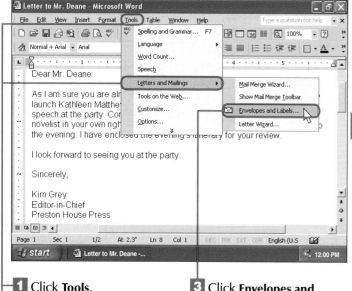

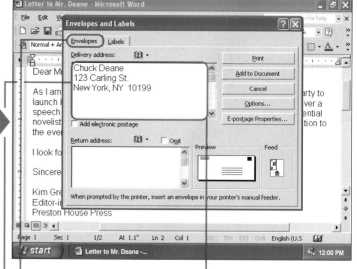

1 Click **Tools**.

2 Click **Letters and Mailings**.

3 Click **Envelopes and Labels**.

■ The Envelopes and Labels dialog box appears.

4 Click the **Envelopes** tab.

■ This area displays the delivery address. If Word finds an address in your document, Word will enter the address for you.

5 To enter a delivery address, click this area. Then type the delivery address.

Note: To remove any existing text before typing a delivery address, drag the mouse I over the text until you highlight the text. Then press the Delete *key.*

When would I omit the return address from an envelope?

You would omit the return address if your envelope already displays a return address. Company stationery often displays a return address.

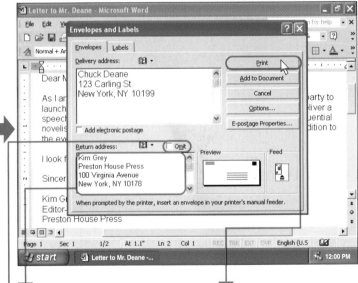

Can I make an envelope part of my document?

Yes. To make an envelope part of your document, perform steps **1** to **9** below, except click the **Add to Document** button in step **8**. The envelope appears before the first page in your document. You can edit, format, save and print the envelope as part of your document.

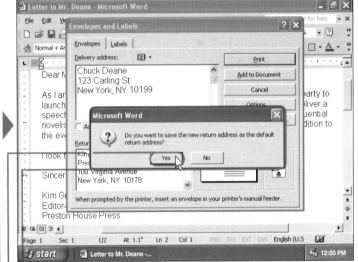

6 To enter a return address, click this area. Then type the return address.

7 If you do not want to print a return address, click **Omit** (☐ changes to ☑).

8 Click **Print** to print the envelope.

■ This dialog box appears if you entered a return address.

9 To save the return address, click **Yes**.

■ If you save the return address, the address will appear as the return address each time you print an envelope. This saves you from having to retype the address.

PRINT LABELS

You can use Word to print labels. Labels are useful for addressing envelopes, creating name tags, labeling file folders and more.

PRINT LABELS

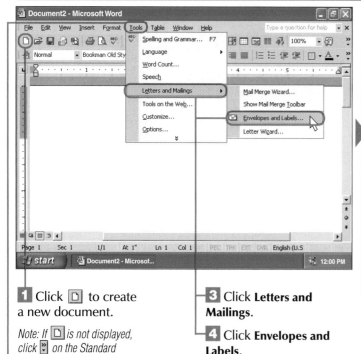

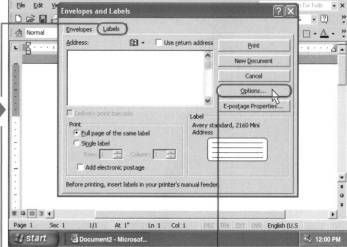

1 Click 🗋 to create a new document.

Note: If 🗋 is not displayed, click ⇩ on the Standard toolbar to display the button.

2 Click **Tools**.

3 Click **Letters and Mailings**.

4 Click **Envelopes and Labels**.

■ The Envelopes and Labels dialog box appears.

5 Click the **Labels** tab.

6 Click **Options** to select the type of label you will use.

■ The Label Options dialog box appears.

What types of printers can I use to print labels?

Word can set up labels to print on dot matrix, laser and ink jet printers. If you are not sure which type of printer you have, you can consult the documentation included with the printer.

Dot Matrix Laser Ink Jet

Which label product and type should I choose?

You can check your label packaging to determine which label product and type you should choose when printing labels.

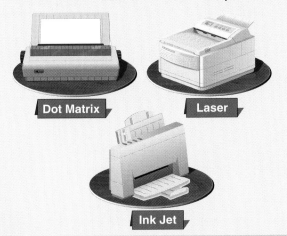

7 Click an option to specify the type of printer you will use to print the labels (○ changes to ⊙).

■ This area displays the printer tray that will contain the labels. You can click this area to specify a different tray.

8 Click this area to display a list of the available label products.

9 Click the label product you will use.

■ This area displays the types of labels available for the label product you selected.

10 Click the type of label you will use.

■ This area displays information about the type of label you selected.

11 Click **OK** to confirm your selections.

CONTINUED

139

After you specify the type of label you will use, Word can add the labels to a new document. You can then enter the information you want to appear on each label.

Ms. Spencer
6757 Main Street
Las Vegas, NV 89199

PRINT LABELS (CONTINUED)

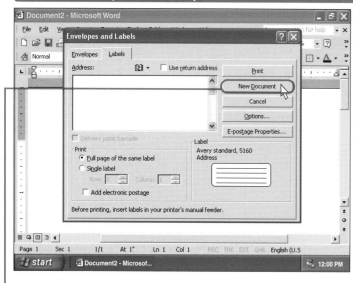

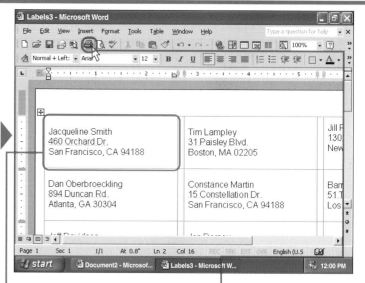

12 Click **New Document** to add the labels to a new document.

■ The labels appear in a new document.

13 Click a label where you want to enter text and then type the text. Repeat this step for each label.

Note: You can format the text on the labels as you would format any text in a document. To format text, see pages 78 to 86.

14 Click 🖨 to print the labels.

Note: If 🖨 is not displayed, click ⋮ on the Standard toolbar to display the button.

Should I save the labels I created?

If you want to be able to edit and print the labels in the future, you should save the labels you created. To save the document containing the labels, see page 22.

Can I quickly create a label for each person on my mailing list?

You can use the Mail Merge Wizard included with Word to quickly create a label for each person on your mailing list. For information on using the Mail Merge Wizard to create labels, see page 194.

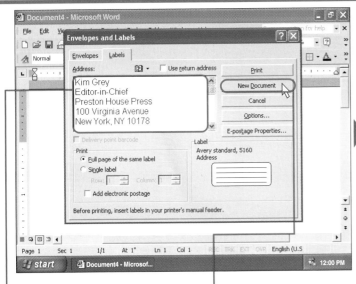

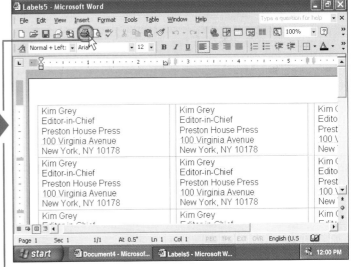

PRINT THE SAME INFORMATION ON EVERY LABEL

1 Perform steps **1** to **11**, starting on page 138.

2 Click this area and then type the information you want to appear on every label.

3 Click **New Document** to add the labels to a new document.

■ The labels appear in a new document. Each label displays the same information.

4 Click 🖨 to print the labels.

Note: If 🖨 is not displayed, click ▶ on the Standard toolbar to display the button.

CHAPTER 8

WORK WITH TABLES

Do you want to learn how to display information in a table? This chapter teaches you how to create and work with tables.

CREATE A TABLE

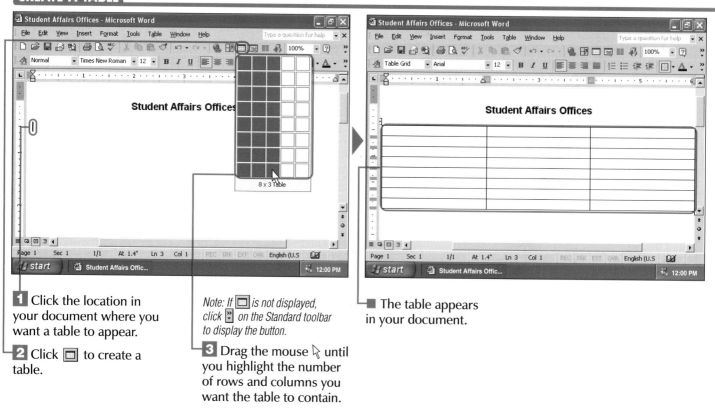

1 Click the location in your document where you want a table to appear.

2 Click ▦ to create a table.

Note: If ▦ is not displayed, click ⁀ on the Standard toolbar to display the button.

3 Drag the mouse ⬚ until you highlight the number of rows and columns you want the table to contain.

■ The table appears in your document.

144

What are the parts of a table?

A table consists of rows, columns and cells.

Row

Column

Cell

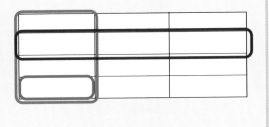

Can I change the appearance of text in a table?

Yes. You can format text in a table as you would format any text in your document. For example, you can change the font, size, color and alignment of text in a table. To format text, see pages 78 to 87.

Pianist	Age	Song
Kate Roberts	12	Mary Had a Little Lamb
Morgan Brown	10	Twinkle, Twinkle, Little Star
Patrick O'Reilly	12	On Top of Old Smokey

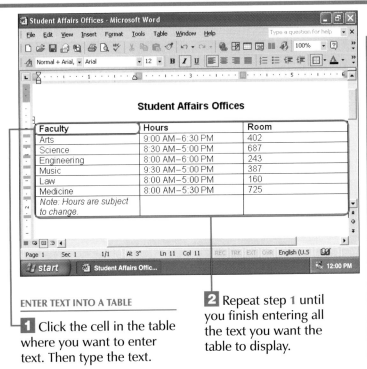

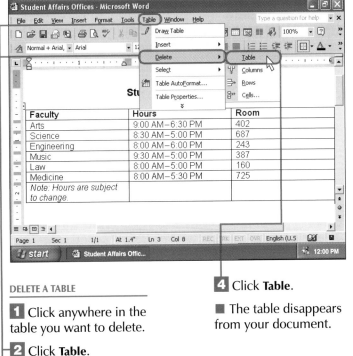

ENTER TEXT INTO A TABLE

1 Click the cell in the table where you want to enter text. Then type the text.

2 Repeat step **1** until you finish entering all the text you want the table to display.

DELETE A TABLE

1 Click anywhere in the table you want to delete.

2 Click **Table**.

3 Click **Delete**.

4 Click **Table**.

■ The table disappears from your document.

ADD A ROW OR COLUMN

You can add a row or column to your table to insert additional information.

ADD A ROW

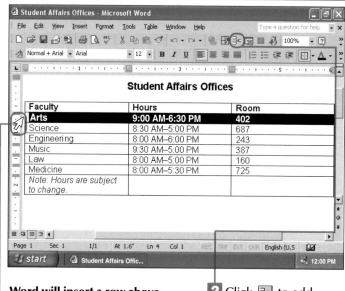

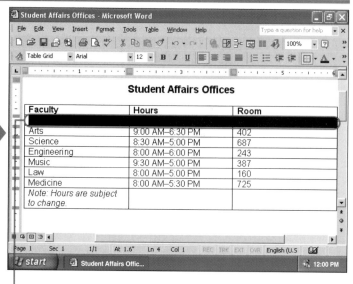

Word will insert a row above the row you select.

1 To select a row, position the mouse I to the left of the row (I changes to ⟋). Then click to select the row.

2 Click ⊞ to add a row to the table.

Note: If ⊞ is not displayed, click ⟩ on the Standard toolbar to display the button.

■ The new row appears in your table.

■ To deselect a row, click outside the selected area.

How do I add a row to the bottom of a table?

To add a row to the bottom of a table, click the bottom right cell in the table. Then press the `Tab` key.

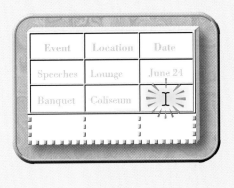

How do I add a column to the right of the last column in a table?

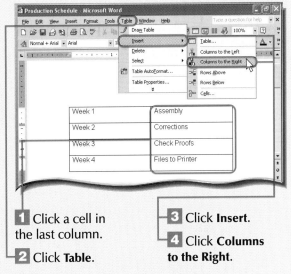

1 Click a cell in the last column.

2 Click **Table**.

3 Click **Insert**.

4 Click **Columns to the Right**.

ADD A COLUMN

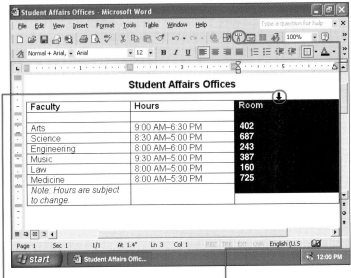

Word will insert a column to the left of the column you select.

1 To select a column, position the mouse I above the column (I changes to ↓). Then click to select the column.

2 Click 🔠 to add a column.

Note: If 🔠 is not displayed, click 🔽 on the Standard toolbar to display the button.

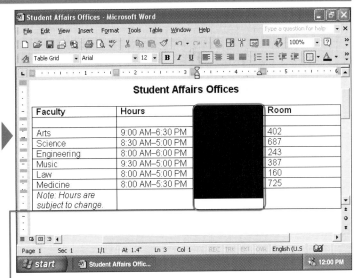

■ The new column appears in your table.

■ To deselect a column, click outside the selected area.

DELETE A ROW OR COLUMN

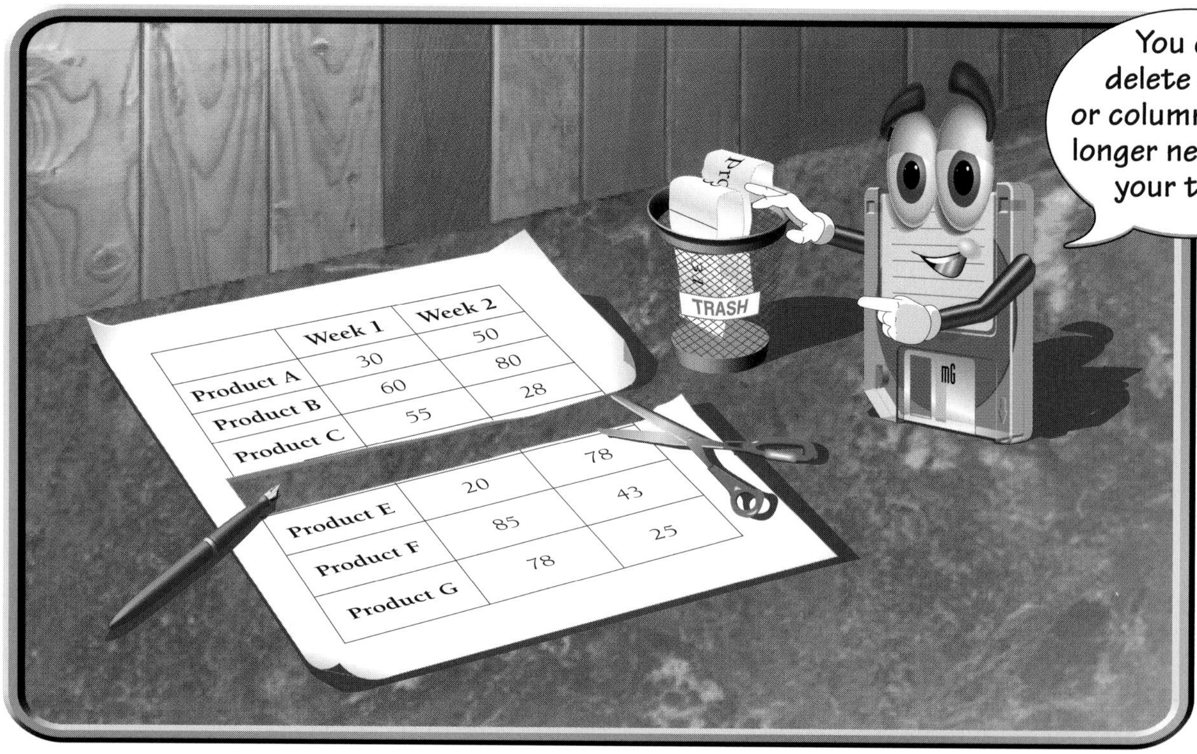

Deleting a row or column will also delete all the information in the row or column.

DELETE A ROW

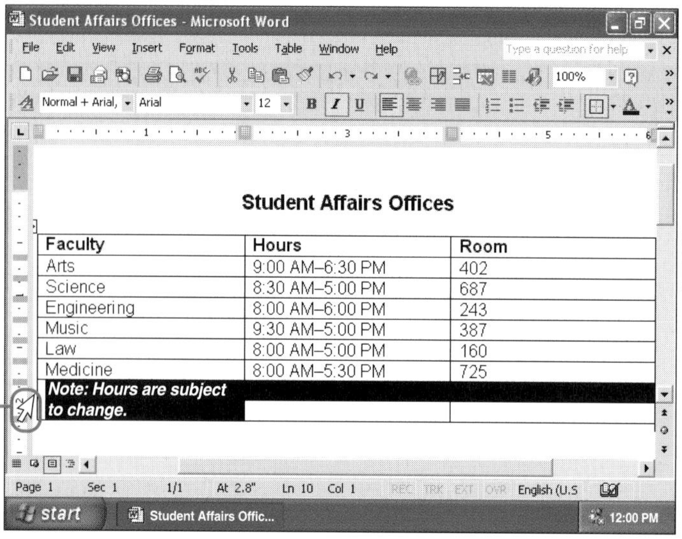

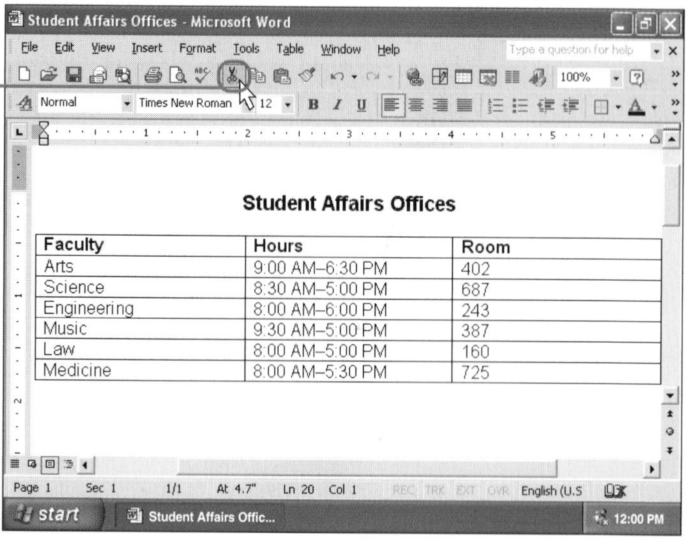

1 To select the row you want to delete, position the mouse I to the left of the row (I changes to ↗). Then click to select the row.

2 Click ✂ to delete the row.

Note: If ✂ is not displayed, click » on the Standard toolbar to display the button.

■ The row disappears from your table.

Can I delete the information in a
row or column without removing
the row or column from my table?

Yes. To select the cells in your table that
contain the information you want to
delete, drag the mouse I over the cells
until you highlight the cells. Then press
the Delete key to remove the information.

How can I restore a row or column
I accidentally deleted?

If you accidentally delete a row or column,
you can click the Undo button (🔄) to
immediately restore the row or column
to your table. For more information on
the Undo feature, see page 51.

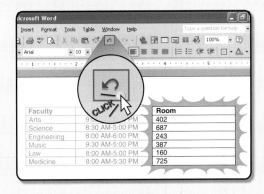

DELETE A COLUMN

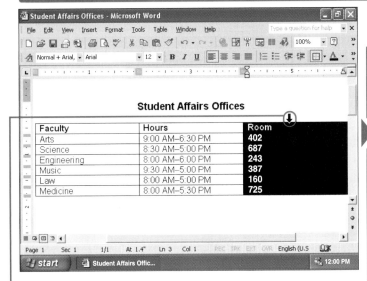

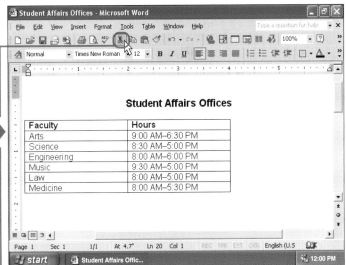

1 To select the column
you want to delete,
position the mouse I
above the column
(I changes to ↓). Then
click to select the column.

2 Click ✂ to delete
the column.

*Note: If ✂ is not displayed,
click ⋮ on the Standard toolbar
to display the button.*

■ The column disappears
from your table.

CHANGE ROW HEIGHT OR COLUMN WIDTH

You can change the height of rows and the width of columns to improve the layout of your table.

CHANGE ROW HEIGHT

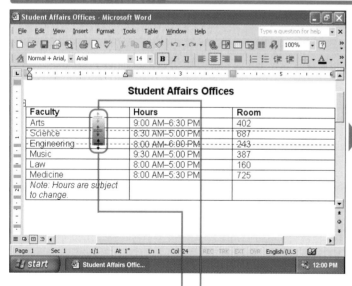

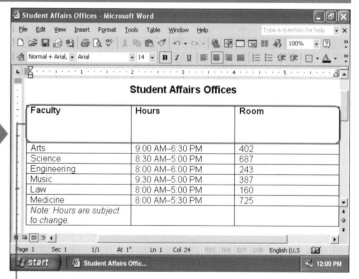

■ You can change a row height only when your document is displayed in the Print Layout or Web Layout view. To change the view of a document, see page 36.

1 Position the mouse I over the bottom edge of the row you want to change to a new height (I changes to ⬍).

2 Drag the row edge to a new position.

■ A dotted line shows the new position.

■ The row displays the new height.

Note: When you change the height of a row, the height of the entire table changes.

Can Word automatically adjust a row height or column width?

Yes. When you enter text into a table, Word automatically increases the row height or column width to accommodate the text you type.

Can I change the column width for only a few cells in a column?

Yes. To select the cells you want to change, position the mouse I over the first cell and then drag the mouse until you highlight all the cells you want to change in the column. To change the width of the selected cells, perform steps **1** and **2** on page 151.

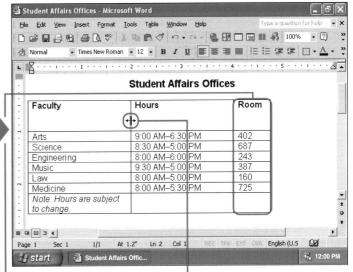

CHANGE COLUMN WIDTH

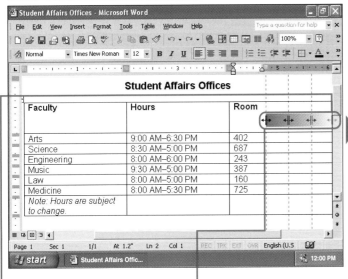

1 Position the mouse I over the right edge of the column you want to change to a new width (I changes to ↔).

2 Drag the column edge to a new position.

■ A dotted line shows the new position.

■ The column displays the new width.

Note: When you change the width of a column, the width of the neighboring column also changes. When you change the width of the last column, the width of the entire table changes.

FIT LONGEST ITEM

1 To quickly change a column width to fit the longest item in the column, double-click the right edge of the column.

COMBINE CELLS

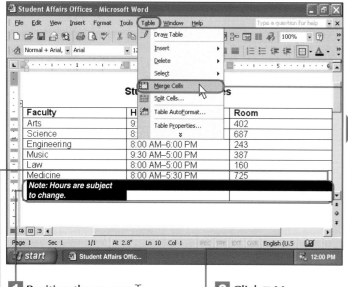

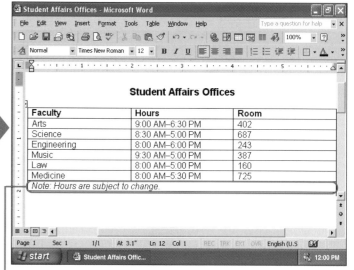

1 Position the mouse I over the first cell you want to combine with other cells.

2 Drag the mouse I until you highlight all the cells you want to combine.

3 Click **Table**.

4 Click **Merge Cells**.

Note: If Merge Cells does not appear on the menu, position the mouse ℝ over the bottom of the menu to display all the menu options.

■ The cells combine to create one large cell.

■ To deselect cells, click outside the selected area.

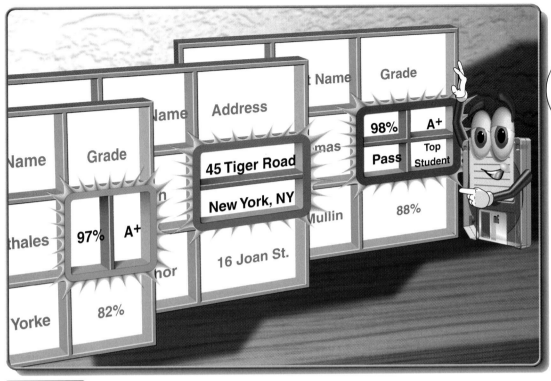

You can split one cell in your table into two or more cells.

You can split a cell into columns, rows or both columns and rows.

Split Cell into Columns

Split Cell into Rows

Split Cell into Columns and Rows

SPLIT CELLS

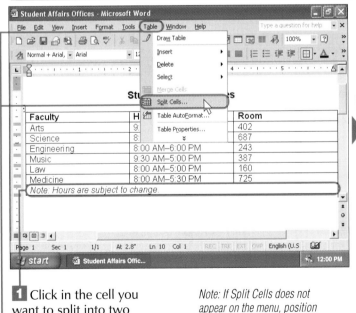

1 Click in the cell you want to split into two or more cells.

2 Click **Table**.

3 Click **Split Cells**.

Note: If Split Cells does not appear on the menu, position the mouse ⌖ over the bottom of the menu to display all the menu options.

■ The Split Cells dialog box appears.

4 Double-click the number in this area and type the number of columns you want to split the cell into.

5 Double-click the number in this area and type the number of rows you want to split the cell into.

6 Click **OK** to split the cell.

FORMAT A TABLE

Word offers many ready-to-use designs that you can choose from to quickly give your table a professional appearance.

FORMAT A TABLE

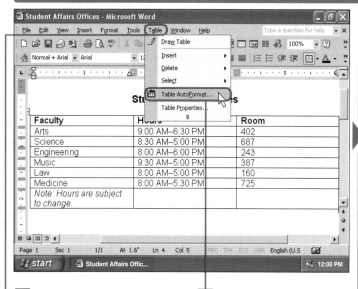

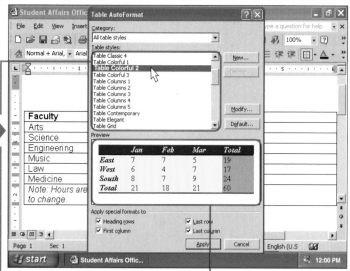

1 Click anywhere in the table you want to format.

2 Click **Table**.

3 Click **Table AutoFormat**.

■ The Table AutoFormat dialog box appears.

■ This area displays a list of the available table designs.

4 Click the table design you want to use.

■ This area displays a sample of the table design you selected.

Note: To display a sample of a different table design, repeat step 4.

What parts of a table can Word apply special formats to?

Word can apply special formats to the heading rows, the first column, the last row and the last column of a table. For example, Word can **bold text** in the heading rows of a table or apply borders to the last row of a table.

Salesperson	January	February	March	Total
Joe	25	12	44	81
Dana	36	22	32	90
John	24	54	36	114
Marie	29	21	42	92
Total	114	109	154	377

Heading Row · **First Column** · **Last Column** · **Last Row**

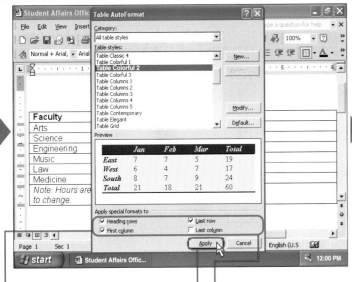

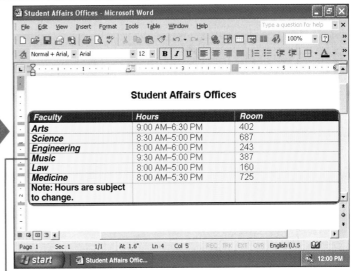

◼ This area displays the parts of the table that Word can apply special formats to.

◼ A check mark (✔) beside an option indicates that Word will apply special formats to that part of the table.

5 To add (☑) or remove (☐) a check mark beside an option, click the option.

6 Click **Apply** or press the Enter key to apply the design to your table.

◼ The table displays the design you selected.

◼ To remove a table design from a table, repeat steps **1** to **4**, selecting **Table Grid** in step **4**. Then press the Enter key.

CHAPTER 9

WORK WITH GRAPHICS

Are you interested in using graphics to enhance the appearance of your document? This chapter shows you how.

Drawing Canvas

mG

ADD AN AUTOSHAPE

Word provides a group of ready-made shapes, called AutoShapes, that you can add to your document.

Word offers several types of AutoShapes such as lines, arrows, stars and banners.

Word can display AutoShapes only in the Print Layout and Web Layout views. To change the view of a document, see page 36.

ADD AN AUTOSHAPE

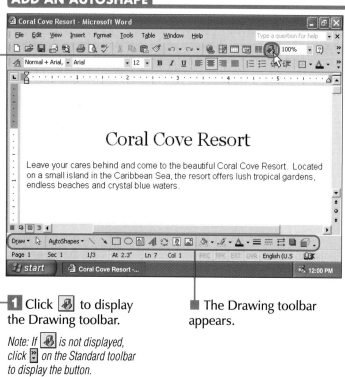

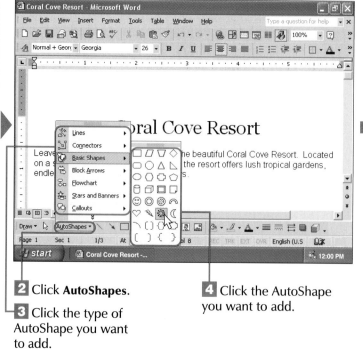

1 Click 🔲 to display the Drawing toolbar.

Note: If 🔲 is not displayed, click ⋙ on the Standard toolbar to display the button.

■ The Drawing toolbar appears.

2 Click **AutoShapes**.

3 Click the type of AutoShape you want to add.

4 Click the AutoShape you want to add.

How can I add text to an AutoShape?

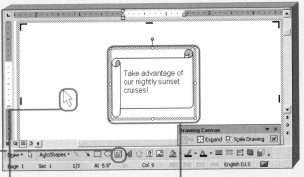

1 Click a blank area beside the AutoShape to display the drawing canvas.

2 Click on the Drawing toolbar.

Note: If you are adding text to an AutoShape from the Callouts category, do not perform steps 1 and 2.

3 Click the AutoShape you want to display text and then type the text.

4 When you finish typing the text, click outside the AutoShape.

How do I delete an AutoShape?

To delete an AutoShape, click an edge of the AutoShape and then press the Delete key.

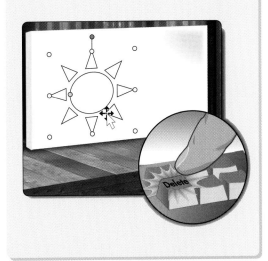

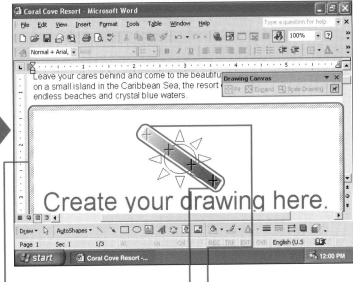

■ Word adds a drawing canvas to your document. A drawing canvas provides an area that allows you to arrange graphics and move several graphics at once.

Note: For more information on using a drawing canvas, see page 172.

5 Position the mouse + where you want to begin drawing the AutoShape.

6 Drag the mouse + until the AutoShape is the size you want.

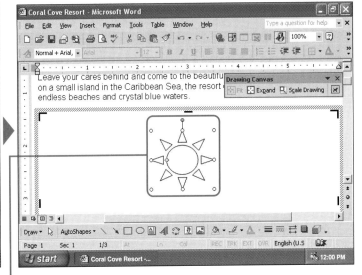

■ The AutoShape appears. The handles (o) around the AutoShape allow you to change the size of the AutoShape. To move or resize an AutoShape, see page 168 or 169.

■ To deselect an AutoShape, click outside the AutoShape.

■ To hide the drawing canvas, click outside the drawing canvas or press the Esc key.

Note: To hide the Drawing toolbar, repeat step 1.

ADD WORDART

You can add WordArt to your document to display a decorative title or draw attention to important information.

ADD WORDART

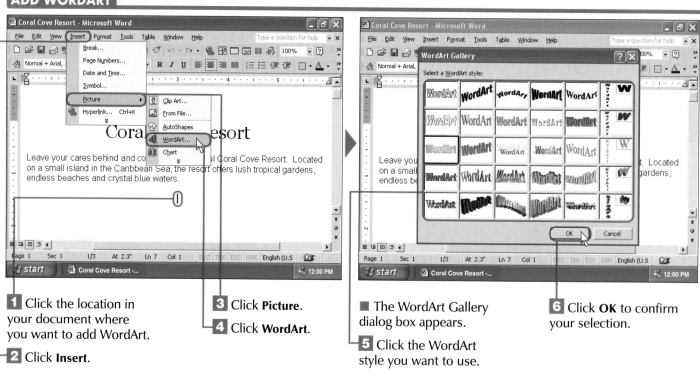

1 Click the location in your document where you want to add WordArt.

2 Click **Insert**.

3 Click **Picture**.

4 Click **WordArt**.

■ The WordArt Gallery dialog box appears.

5 Click the WordArt style you want to use.

6 Click **OK** to confirm your selection.

How do I edit WordArt text?

To edit WordArt text, double-click the WordArt to redisplay the Edit WordArt Text dialog box. Then perform steps 7 and 8 below to specify the new text you want the WordArt to display.

How can I change the appearance of WordArt?

When you click WordArt, the WordArt toolbar appears, displaying buttons that allow you to change the appearance of the WordArt. For example, you can click ⬜ to display all the letters in the WordArt at the same height.

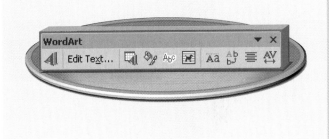

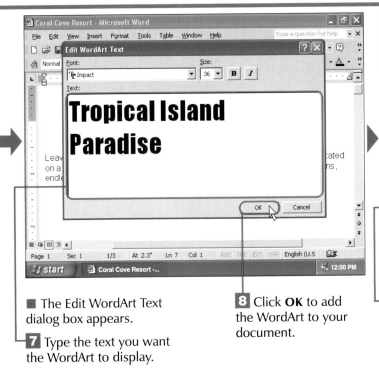

■ The Edit WordArt Text dialog box appears.

7 Type the text you want the WordArt to display.

8 Click **OK** to add the WordArt to your document.

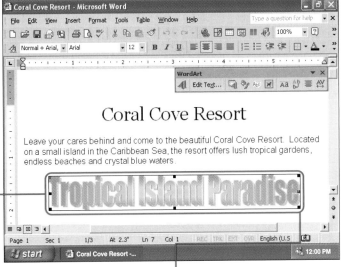

■ The WordArt appears in your document.

Note: To move or resize WordArt, see page 168 or 169.

DELETE WORDART

1 Click the WordArt you want to delete. Handles (■) appear around the WordArt.

2 Press the Delete key to delete the WordArt.

You can add a picture to your document to illustrate a concept or enhance the appearance of the document.

Word can display pictures only in the Print Layout and Web Layout views. To change the view of a document, see page 36.

ADD A PICTURE

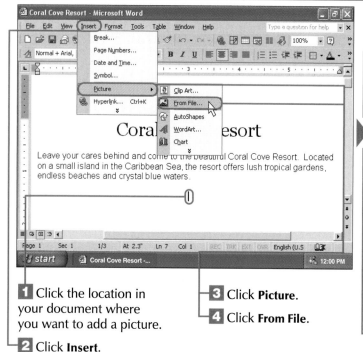

1 Click the location in your document where you want to add a picture.

2 Click **Insert**.

3 Click **Picture**.

4 Click **From File**.

■ The Insert Picture dialog box appears.

■ This area shows the location of the displayed pictures. You can click this area to change the location.

■ This area allows you to access pictures stored in commonly used locations. You can click a location to display the pictures stored in the location.

Note: For information on the commonly used locations, see the top of page 23.

Where can I get pictures that I can add to my documents?

You can purchase collections of pictures at computer stores or obtain pictures on the Internet. You can also use a scanner to scan pictures into your computer or create your own pictures using an image editing program, such as Jasc Paint Shop Pro.

How can I change the appearance of a picture?

When you click a picture, the Picture toolbar appears, displaying buttons that allow you to change the appearance of the picture. For example, you can click [☼↑] or [☼↓] to increase or decrease the brightness of the picture.

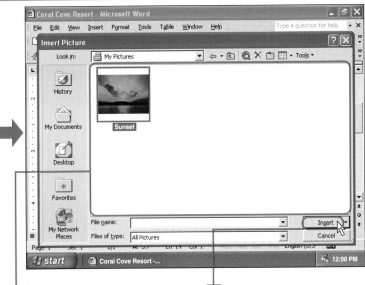

5 Click the picture you want to add to your document.

6 Click **Insert** to add the picture to your document.

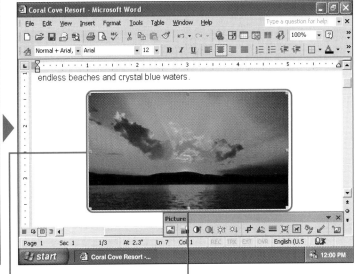

■ The picture appears in your document.

Note: To move or resize a picture, see page 168 or 169.

DELETE A PICTURE

1 Click the picture you want to delete. Handles (■) appear around the picture.

2 Press the Delete key to delete the picture.

ADD A CLIP ART IMAGE

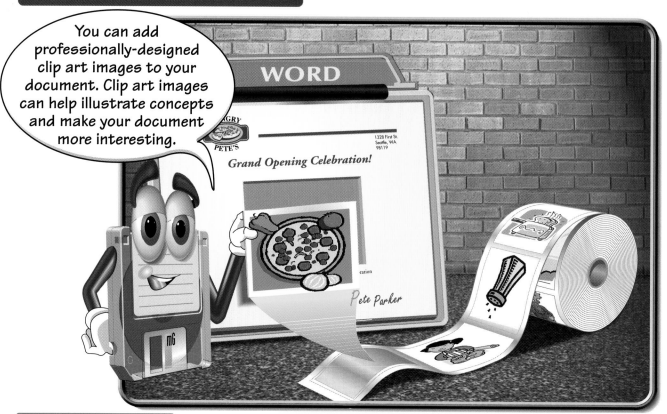

You can add professionally-designed clip art images to your document. Clip art images can help illustrate concepts and make your document more interesting.

ADD A CLIP ART IMAGE

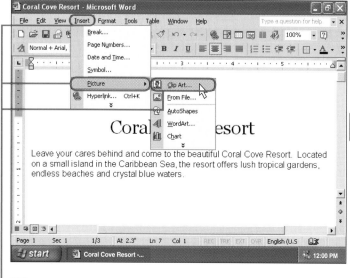

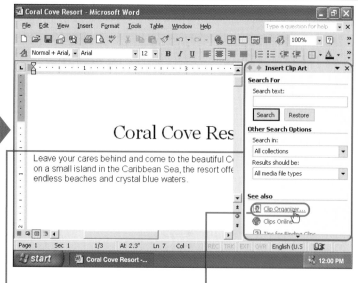

1 Click **Insert**.

2 Click **Picture**.

3 Click **Clip Art**.

*Note: The first time you add a clip art image to a document, the Add Clips to Organizer dialog box appears. Click **Now** in the dialog box to catalog the image, sound and video files on your computer.*

■ The Insert Clip Art task pane appears.

4 Click **Clip Organizer** to view the image, sound and video files in the Clip Organizer.

■ The Microsoft Clip Organizer window appears.

How does the Clip Organizer arrange
image, sound and video files?

The Clip Organizer arranges media files
into three main folders.

My Collections

Displays the media files you
have specified as your favorites
and media files that came with
Microsoft Windows.

Office Collections

Displays the media files that
came with Microsoft Office.

Web Collections

Displays the media files that
are available at Microsoft's
Web site and Web sites in
partnership with Microsoft.

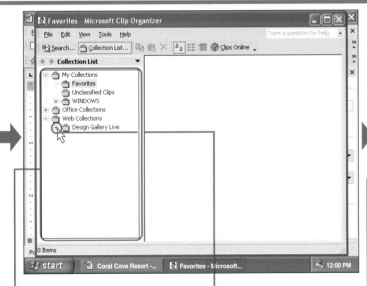

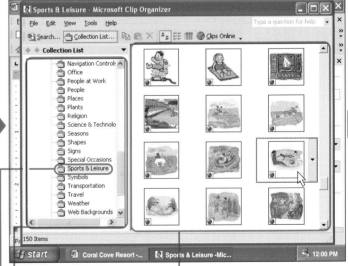

■ This area lists the folders
containing image, sound and
video files that you can add
to your document.

■ A folder displaying a plus
sign (⊞) contains hidden
folders.

5 To display the hidden
folders within a folder, click
a plus sign (⊞) beside a
folder (⊞ changes to ⊟).

*Note: You must be connected to the
Internet to view the contents of the
Web Collections folder.*

■ The hidden folders
appear.

*Note: To once again hide the
folders within a folder, click a
minus sign (⊟) beside a folder.*

6 Click a folder of
interest.

■ This area displays the
contents of the folder you
selected.

7 Click the image you want
to add to your document.

CONTINUED ▶

ADD A CLIP ART IMAGE

After you locate an image you want to add to your document, you can copy the image and then place the image in your document.

ADD A CLIP ART IMAGE (CONTINUED)

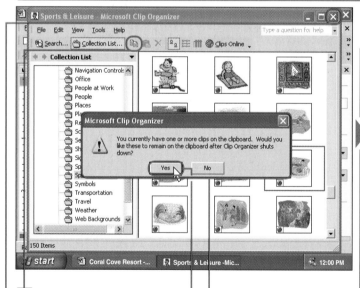

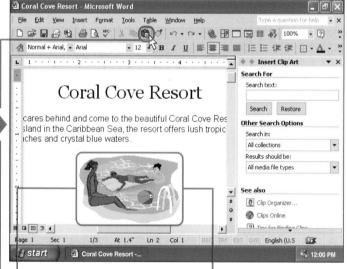

8 Click 🖻 to copy the image you selected.

9 Click ✕ to close the Microsoft Clip Organizer window.

■ A dialog box appears, stating that you have one or more clip art images on the clipboard.

Note: The clipboard temporarily stores information you have selected to move or copy.

10 Click **Yes** to keep the image on the clipboard.

11 Click the location in your document where you want to add the image.

12 Click 🖻 to place the image in your document.

■ The image appears in your document.

Note: To move or resize an image, see page 168 or 169.

Where can I obtain more clip art images?

You can buy collections of clip art images at computer stores. Many Web sites, such as www.allfree-clipart.com and www.noeticart.com, also offer clip art images you can use in your documents.

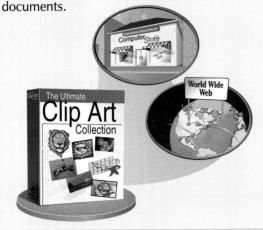

How do I delete a clip art image?

To delete a clip art image, click the clip art image and then press the `Delete` key.

SEARCH FOR A CLIP ART IMAGE

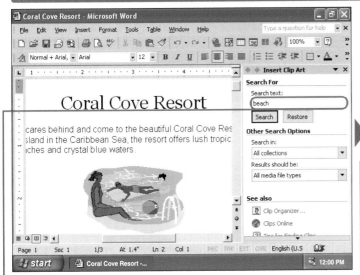

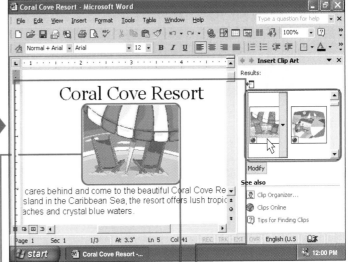

You can search for clip art images by specifying one or more words of interest.

1 Click this area and then type one or more words that describe the clip art image you want to find. Then press the `Enter` key.

Note: If the Insert Clip Art task pane is not displayed, perform steps 1 to 3 on page 164 to display the task pane.

■ This area displays the images that match the words you specified.

2 Click the location in your document where you want to add an image.

3 Click the image you want to add to your document.

■ The image appears in your document.

Note: To move or resize an image, see page 168 or 169.

167

You can change the location of a graphic in your document.

Word can display all types of graphics in the Print Layout and Web Layout views. To change the view of a document, see page 36.

MOVE A GRAPHIC

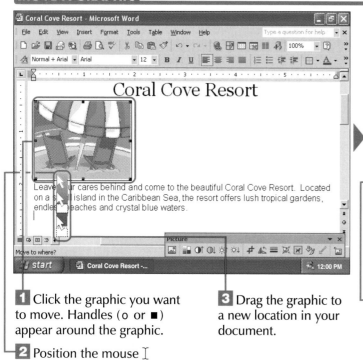

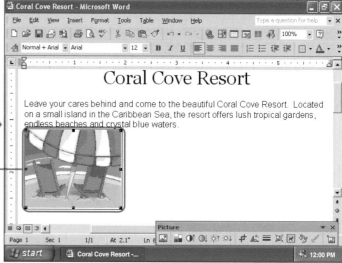

1 Click the graphic you want to move. Handles (o or ■) appear around the graphic.

2 Position the mouse I over an edge of the graphic (I changes to ⊹ or ⧀).

3 Drag the graphic to a new location in your document.

■ The graphic appears in the new location.

■ To deselect the graphic, click outside the graphic.

> You can change the size of a graphic in your document.

Word can display all types of graphics in the Print Layout and Web Layout views. To change the view of a document, see page 36.

RESIZE A GRAPHIC

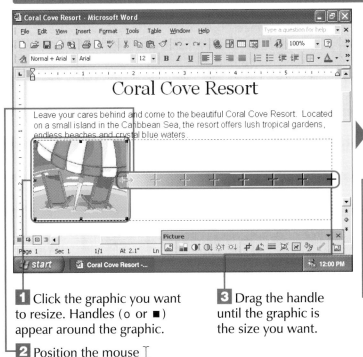

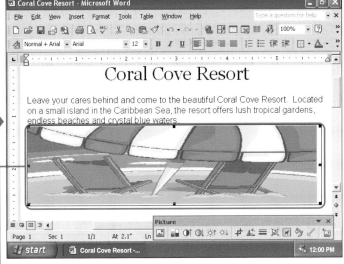

1 Click the graphic you want to resize. Handles (o or ■) appear around the graphic.

2 Position the mouse I over one of the handles (I changes to ↔, ↕, ↗ or ↘).

3 Drag the handle until the graphic is the size you want.

■ The graphic appears in the new size.

■ To deselect the graphic, click outside the graphic.

CHANGE COLOR OF A GRAPHIC

You can change the color of a graphic in your document.

You cannot change the color of some clip art images and pictures.

CHANGE COLOR OF A GRAPHIC

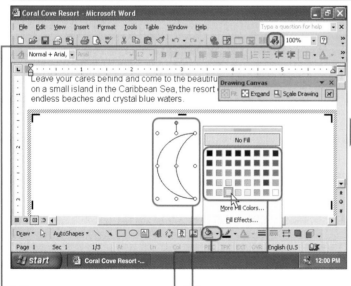

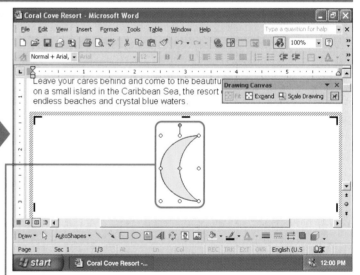

1 Click 🖼 to display the Drawing toolbar.

Note: If 🖼 is not displayed, click ⏩ on the Standard toolbar to display the button.

2 Click the graphic you want to change to a different color. Handles (o or ■) appear around the graphic.

3 Click ⏷ in this area to display the available colors.

4 Click the color you want to use.

■ The graphic appears in the color you selected.

■ To deselect a graphic, click outside the graphic.

Note: To hide the Drawing toolbar, repeat step 1.

170

You can rotate a graphic in your document.

You cannot rotate text boxes and some AutoShapes.

ROTATE A GRAPHIC

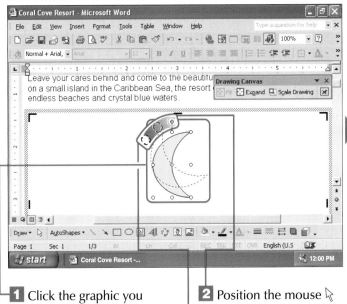

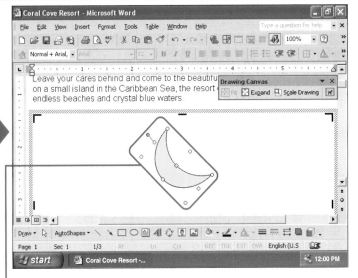

1 Click the graphic you want to rotate. Handles (o) appear around the graphic.

Note: If ■ handles appear around the graphic, you cannot rotate the graphic.

2 Position the mouse ▷ over the green dot (▷ changes to ↻).

3 Drag the mouse ⟡ in the direction you want to rotate the graphic.

■ The graphic appears in the new position.

■ To deselect a graphic, click outside the graphic.

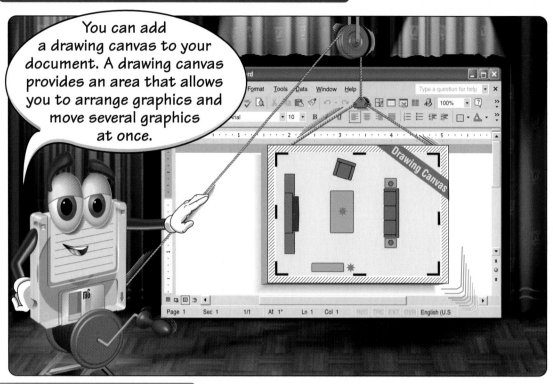

You can add a drawing canvas to your document. A drawing canvas provides an area that allows you to arrange graphics and move several graphics at once.

Word can display a drawing canvas only in the Print Layout and Web Layout views. To change the view of a document, see page 36.

Word automatically creates a drawing canvas when you add some types of graphics to your document, such as AutoShapes and text boxes.

CREATE A DRAWING CANVAS

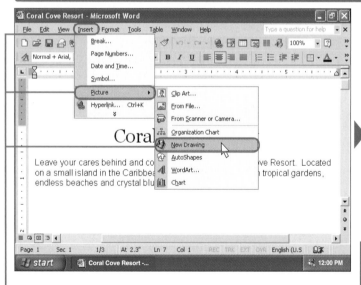

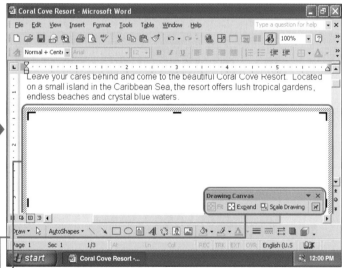

1 Click **Insert**.

2 Click **Picture**.

3 Click **New Drawing**.

Note: If New Drawing does not appear on the menu, position the mouse ⌖ over the bottom of the menu to display all the menu options.

■ A drawing canvas appears in your document.

■ The Drawing Canvas toolbar also appears, displaying buttons you can use to work with the drawing canvas.

Note: If the Drawing Canvas toolbar does not appear, right-click the drawing canvas and then select ***Show Drawing Canvas Toolbar***.

■ You can add graphics, such as an AutoShape, text box or picture, to the drawing canvas.

■ To deselect the drawing canvas, click outside the drawing canvas or press the Esc key.

SIMPLIFY IT

How do I delete a drawing canvas?

To delete a drawing canvas, click a blank area inside the canvas and then press the Delete key. Deleting a drawing canvas will delete all the graphics on the canvas. If you want to keep the graphics, you must move the graphics off the drawing canvas before deleting the canvas. To move a graphic, see page 168.

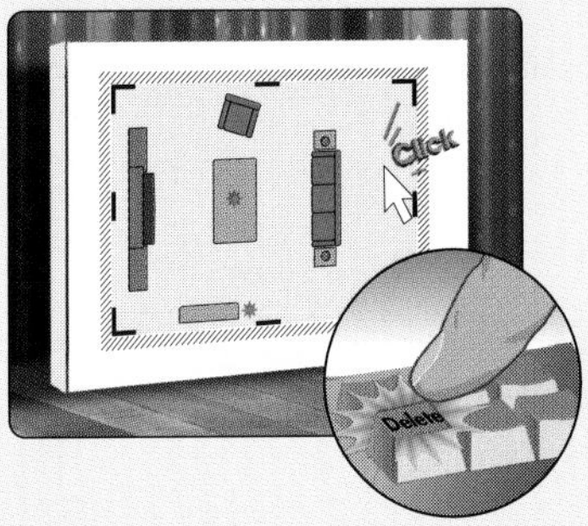

SIMPLIFY IT

How can I change the size of a drawing canvas and the graphics on the canvas at the same time?

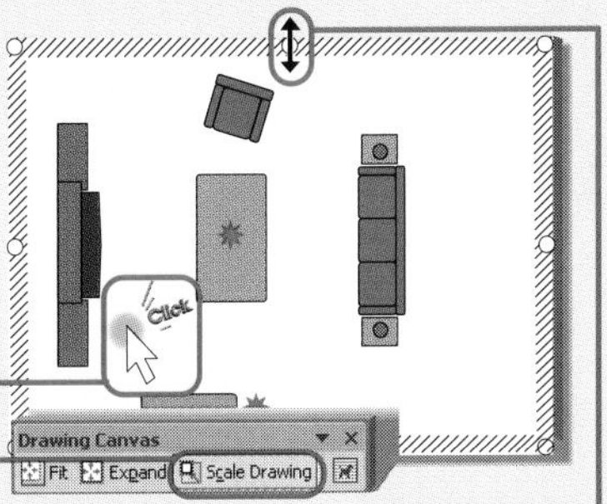

1 Click inside the drawing canvas you want to resize.

2 Click **Scale Drawing**.

3 Position the mouse over a handle (○) on the drawing canvas border and then drag the handle until the canvas and the graphics are the size you want.

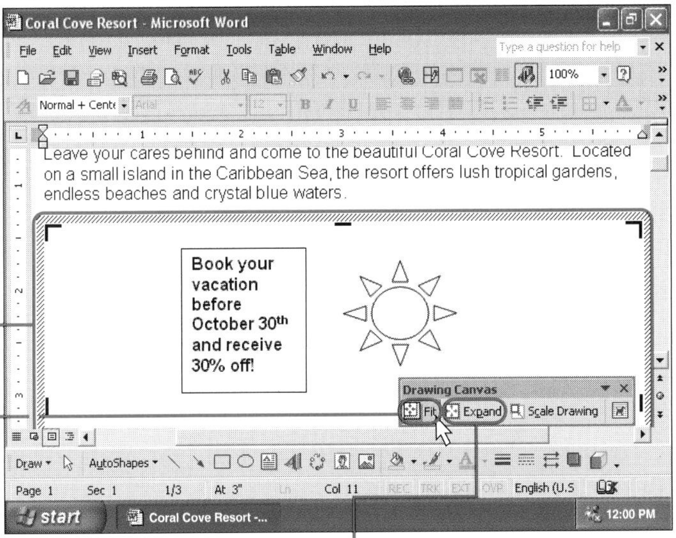

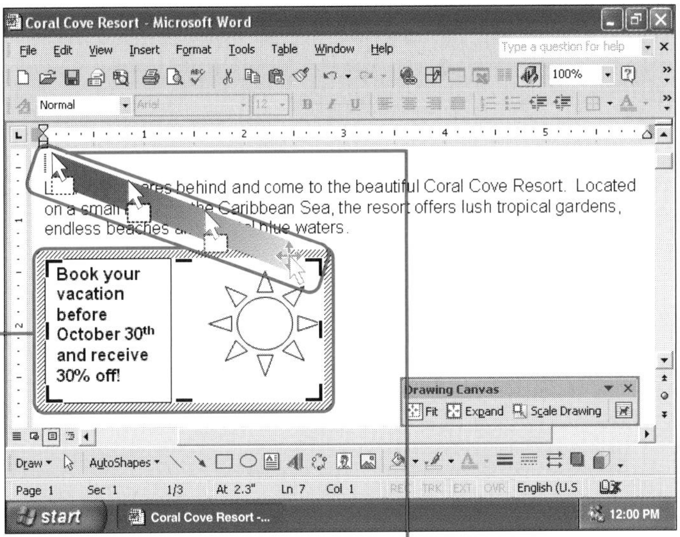

RESIZE A DRAWING CANVAS

1 Click inside the drawing canvas you want to resize.

2 Click **Fit** to make the drawing canvas border fit tightly around the graphics.

Note: The Fit button is only available if you have two or more graphics on the drawing canvas.

■ To enlarge the drawing canvas, click **Expand** until the drawing canvas is the size you want.

MOVE A DRAWING CANVAS

1 Click inside the drawing canvas you want to move.

2 Position the mouse over the border of the drawing canvas (changes to ✥).

3 Drag the drawing canvas to a new location.

Note: The drawing canvas will appear where you position the dotted insertion point on your screen.

WRAP TEXT AROUND A GRAPHIC

After you add a graphic to your document, you can choose how you want to wrap text around the graphic.

WRAP TEXT AROUND A GRAPHIC

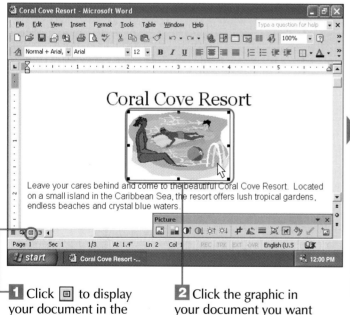

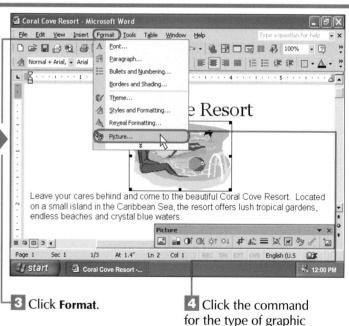

1 Click 🔲 to display your document in the Print Layout view.

2 Click the graphic in your document you want to wrap text around. Handles (o or ▪) appear around the graphic.

Note: For information on wrapping text around a graphic on a drawing canvas, see the top of page 175.

3 Click **Format**.

4 Click the command for the type of graphic you selected, such as **AutoShape**, **Picture** or **WordArt**.

▪ The Format dialog box appears.

How can Word align a graphic with text?

Word can align a graphic to the left, center or right of text.

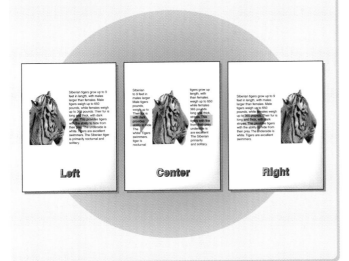

Left   Center   Right

Can I wrap text around a graphic on a drawing canvas?

Yes. To wrap text around a graphic on a drawing canvas, perform steps **1** to **8** below, except click a blank area on the drawing canvas in step **2** and select **Drawing Canvas** in step **4**. For information on using a drawing canvas, see page 172.

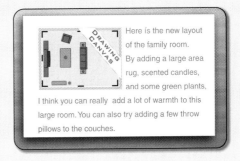

Here is the new layout of the family room. By adding a large area rug, scented candles, and some green plants, I think you can really add a lot of warmth to this large room. You can also try adding a few throw pillows to the couches.

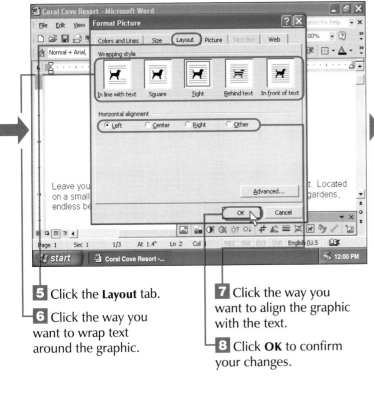

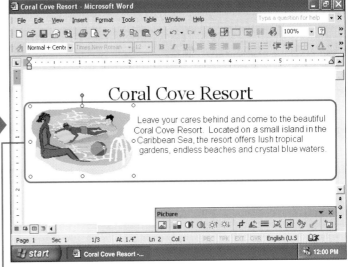

5 Click the **Layout** tab.

6 Click the way you want to wrap text around the graphic.

7 Click the way you want to align the graphic with the text.

8 Click **OK** to confirm your changes.

■ The text wraps around the graphic.

■ To deselect a graphic, click outside the graphic.

175

You can add a diagram to a document to illustrate a concept or idea. Word provides several types of diagrams for you to choose from.

Word can display diagrams only in the Print Layout and Web Layout views. To change the view of a document, see page 36.

ADD A DIAGRAM

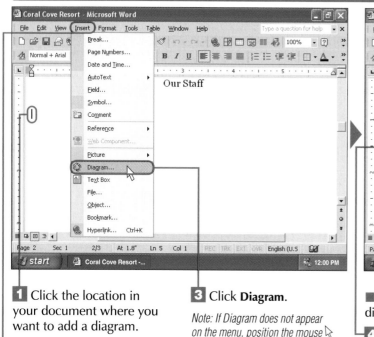

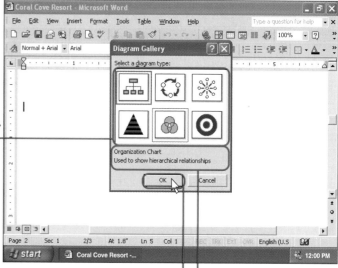

1 Click the location in your document where you want to add a diagram.

2 Click **Insert**.

3 Click **Diagram**.

Note: If Diagram does not appear on the menu, position the mouse over the bottom of the menu to display all the menu options.

■ The Diagram Gallery dialog box appears.

4 Click the type of diagram you want to add to your document.

Note: For information on the types of diagrams, see the top of page 177.

■ This area displays a description of the diagram you selected.

5 Click **OK** to add the diagram to your document.

What types of diagrams can I add to my document?

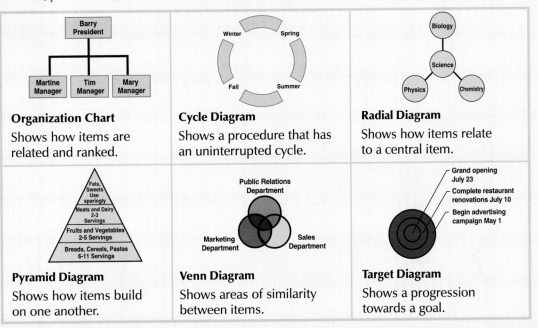

Organization Chart

Shows how items are related and ranked.

Cycle Diagram

Shows a procedure that has an uninterrupted cycle.

Radial Diagram

Shows how items relate to a central item.

Pyramid Diagram

Shows how items build on one another.

Venn Diagram

Shows areas of similarity between items.

Target Diagram

Shows a progression towards a goal.

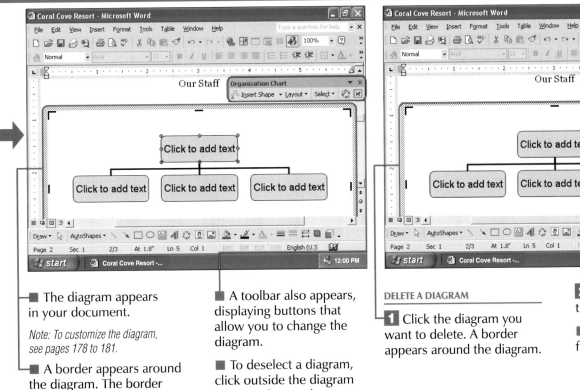

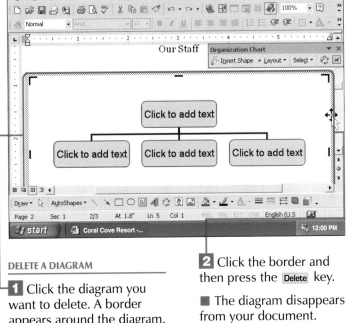

■ The diagram appears in your document.

Note: To customize the diagram, see pages 178 to 181.

■ A border appears around the diagram. The border will not appear when you print your document.

■ A toolbar also appears, displaying buttons that allow you to change the diagram.

■ To deselect a diagram, click outside the diagram or press the Esc key.

DELETE A DIAGRAM

1 Click the diagram you want to delete. A border appears around the diagram.

2 Click the border and then press the Delete key.

■ The diagram disappears from your document.

CONTINUED ▶

ADD A DIAGRAM

You can add text to a diagram to provide descriptions for the shapes in the diagram.

ADD TEXT TO A DIAGRAM

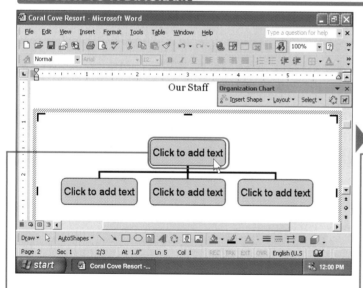

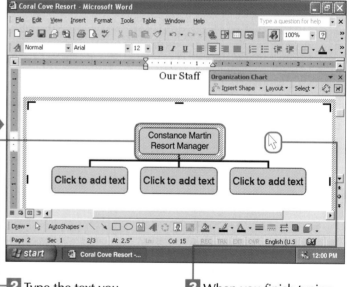

1 To add text to a diagram, click an area that displays the phrase **Click to add text**.

■ A border appears around the area.

2 Type the text you want to add.

3 When you finish typing the text, click outside the text area.

■ You can repeat steps **1** to **3** to add text to another text area in the diagram.

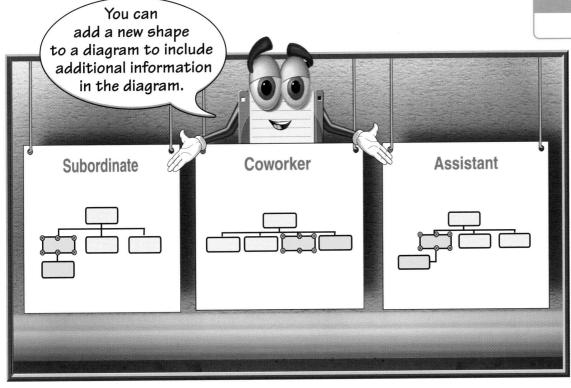

When adding a new shape to an organization chart, there are three types of shapes you can choose from—subordinate, coworker or assistant.

ADD A SHAPE

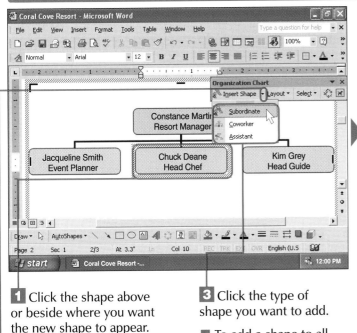

1 Click the shape above or beside where you want the new shape to appear.

2 To add a shape to an organization chart, click ▾ beside **Insert Shape**.

3 Click the type of shape you want to add.

■ To add a shape to all other types of diagrams, click **Insert Shape**.

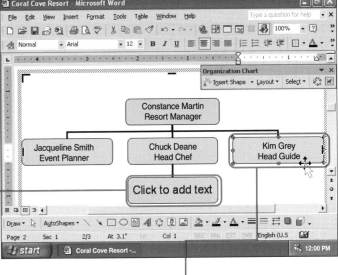

■ A new shape appears in the diagram.

■ You can add text to the text area for new shape.

DELETE A SHAPE

1 Click an edge of the shape you want to delete. Handles (⊗) appear around the shape.

2 Press the Delete key to delete the shape.

CONTINUED

APPLY A DIAGRAM STYLE

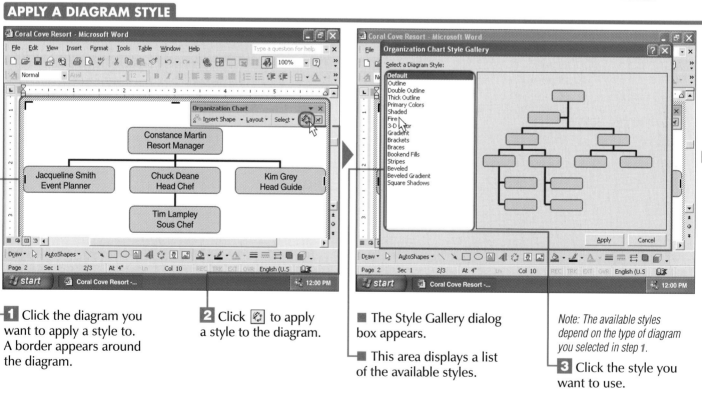

1 Click the diagram you want to apply a style to. A border appears around the diagram.

2 Click to apply a style to the diagram.

■ The Style Gallery dialog box appears.

■ This area displays a list of the available styles.

Note: The available styles depend on the type of diagram you selected in step 1.

3 Click the style you want to use.

Instead of applying a style to a diagram, how can I change the color of only one shape?

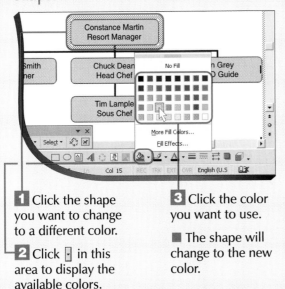

1 Click the shape you want to change to a different color.

2 Click ⏷ in this area to display the available colors.

3 Click the color you want to use.

■ The shape will change to the new color.

How can I change the color of the text in a diagram?

You can change the color of text in a diagram as you would change the color of any text in your document. To change the color of text, see page 82.

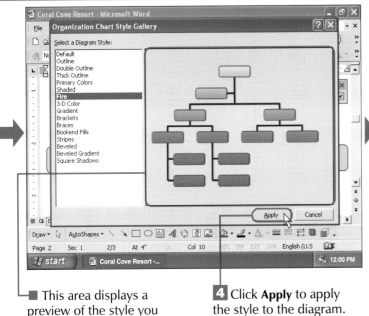

■ This area displays a preview of the style you selected.

Note: You can repeat step 3 to view a preview of a different style.

4 Click **Apply** to apply the style to the diagram.

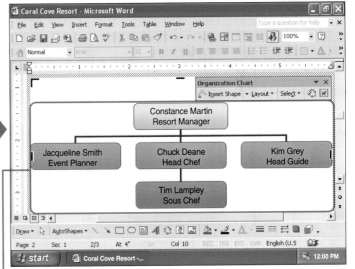

■ The diagram displays the new style.

■ To return to the original diagram style, repeat steps **1** to **4**, selecting **Default** in step **3**.

181

CHAPTER 10

USING MAIL MERGE

Would you like to quickly produce a personalized letter for each person on a mailing list? This chapter teaches you how.

CREATE LETTERS USING MAIL MERGE

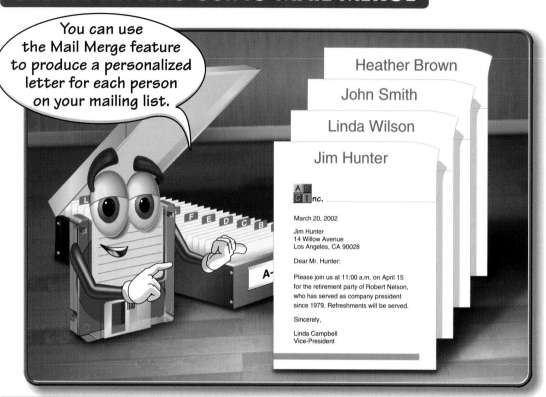

You can use the Mail Merge feature to produce a personalized letter for each person on your mailing list.

Performing a mail merge is useful if you want to send the same document, such as an announcement or advertisement, to many people.

The Mail Merge Wizard guides you step by step through the mail merge process

CREATE LETTERS USING MAIL MERGE

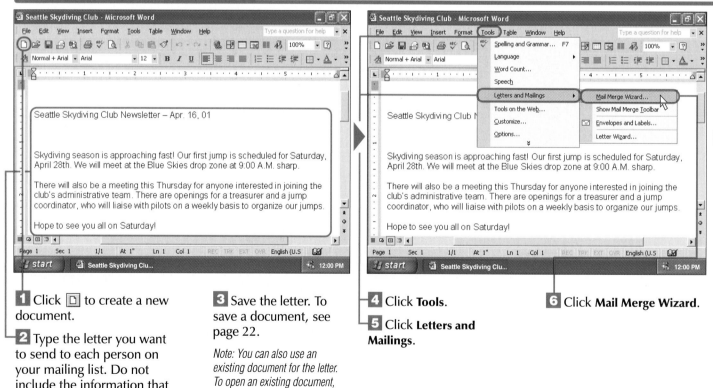

1 Click 🗋 to create a new document.

2 Type the letter you want to send to each person on your mailing list. Do not include the information that will change in each letter, such as a person's name or address.

3 Save the letter. To save a document, see page 22.

Note: You can also use an existing document for the letter. To open an existing document, see page 26.

4 Click **Tools**.

5 Click **Letters and Mailings**.

6 Click **Mail Merge Wizard**.

What other types of documents can I create using the Mail Merge Wizard?

E-mail messages

Creates an e-mail message for each person on your mailing list.

Envelopes

Creates an envelope for each person on your mailing list.

Labels

Creates a label for each person on your mailing list. For information on creating labels using the Mail Merge Wizard, see page 194.

Directory

Creates a document that contains information about each person on your mailing list.

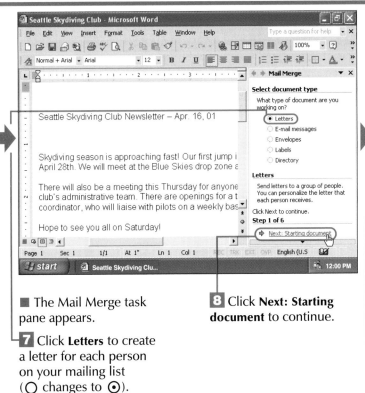

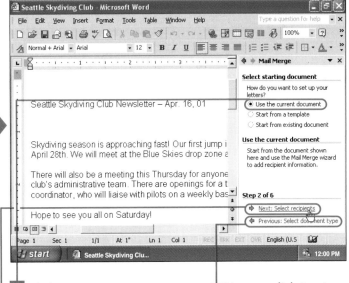

■ The Mail Merge task pane appears.

7 Click **Letters** to create a letter for each person on your mailing list (○ changes to ⊙).

8 Click **Next: Starting document** to continue.

9 Click **Use the current document** to use the displayed document as the letter you will send to each person on your mailing list (○ changes to ⊙).

10 Click **Next: Select recipients** to continue.

■ You can click **Previous** at any time to return to a previous step and change your selections.

CONTINUED

You can specify the address information for each person on your mailing list.

CREATE LETTERS USING MAIL MERGE (CONTINUED)

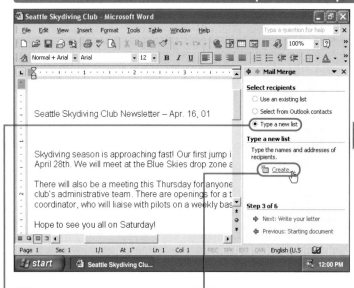

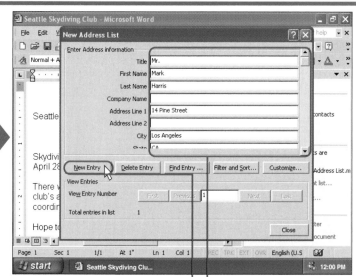

11 Click **Type a new list** to create your mailing list (○ changes to ⊙).

12 Click **Create** to enter the names and addresses of the people on your mailing list.

■ The New Address List dialog box appears, displaying areas where you can enter the information for each person on your mailing list.

13 Click each area and type the appropriate information for a person. You do not have to fill in every area.

14 To enter the information for another person, click **New Entry**.

How can I remove a person I accidentally added to my mailing list?

While creating your mailing list, you can display the information for the person you want to remove and then click the **Delete Entry** button. To confirm the deletion, click **Yes** in the dialog box that appears.

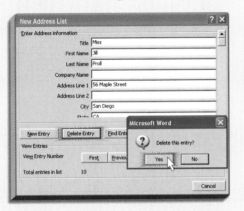

How do I use an existing mailing list to perform a mail merge?

Perform steps 1 to 10 starting on page 184 to begin the mail merge. To select the mailing list you want to use, perform steps 15 to 18 on page 196. Then skip to step 19 on page 188 to continue with the mail merge.

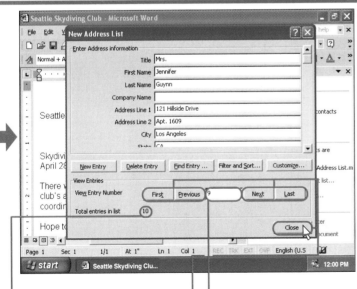

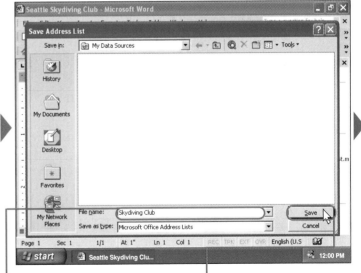

15 Repeat steps 13 and 14 for each person on your mailing list.

■ This area displays the number of people you have added.

■ This area displays the number of the entry that is currently displayed.

■ To browse through the entries, click a button to display the first, previous, next or last entry.

16 When you finish creating your mailing list, click **Close**.

■ The Save Address List dialog box appears.

17 Type a name for the file that will store your mailing list.

18 Click **Save** to save the file.

■ The Mail Merge Recipients dialog box appears.

CONTINUED

When you finish creating your mailing list, Word displays the information for each person on the list. You can select the people you want to receive a personalized letter.

CREATE LETTERS USING MAIL MERGE (CONTINUED)

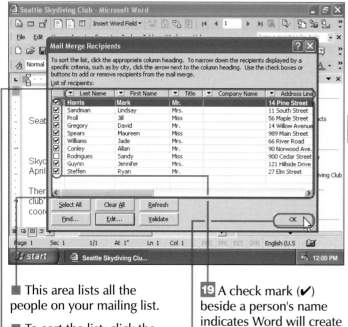

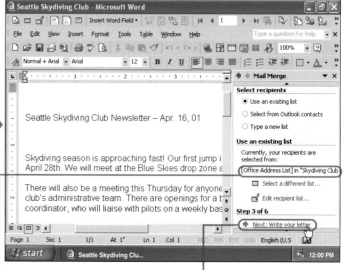

■ This area lists all the people on your mailing list.

■ To sort the list, click the heading of the column you want to use to sort the list.

19 A check mark (✔) beside a person's name indicates Word will create a personalized letter for the person. To add (✔) or remove (☐) a check mark, click the box beside a person's name.

20 Click **OK**.

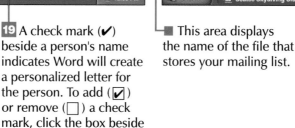

■ This area displays the name of the file that stores your mailing list.

21 Click **Next: Write your letter** to continue.

What type of information can I add to my letters?

Mr. Mark Harris
14 Pine Street
Los Angeles, CA 90023

Address block

Displays the address of a person on your mailing list.

Dear Mr. Harris,

Greeting line

Displays a greeting for a person on your mailing list.

mharris@abccorp.com

More items

Displays a piece of information for a person on your mailing list, such as their home phone number or e-mail address.

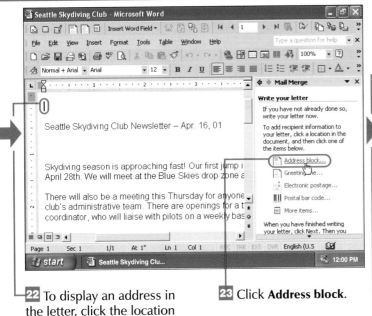

22 To display an address in the letter, click the location in the letter where you want to display the address.

23 Click **Address block**.

■ The Insert Address Block dialog box appears.

24 Click the way you want each person's name to appear in the letter.

■ This area displays a preview of how the address will appear in the letter.

25 Click **OK** to confirm your selection.

CONTINUED ▶

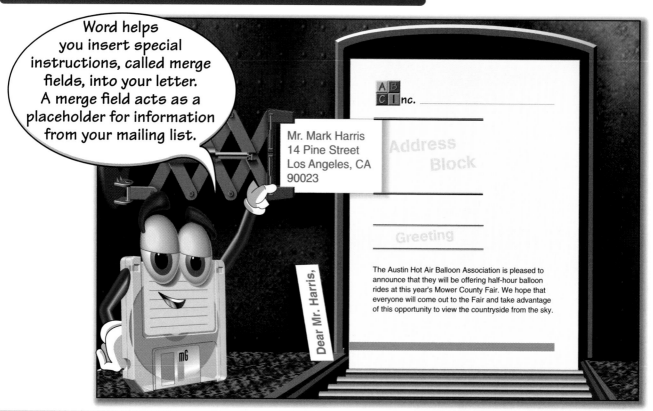

Word helps you insert special instructions, called merge fields, into your letter. A merge field acts as a placeholder for information from your mailing list.

CREATE LETTERS USING MAIL MERGE (CONTINUED)

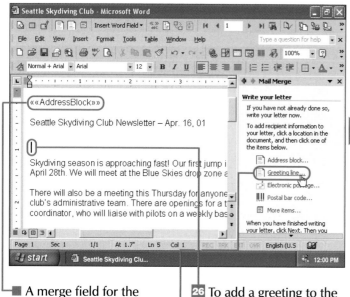

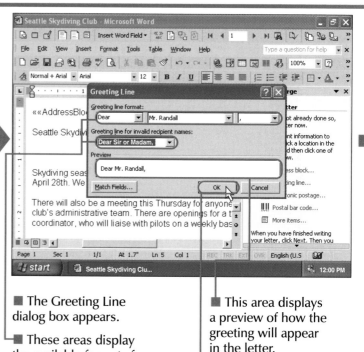

■ A merge field for the address appears in the letter. Word will replace the merge field with an address from your mailing list.

26 To add a greeting to the letter, click the location in the letter where you want to display the greeting.

Note: If you do not want to add a greeting to the letter, skip to step 29.

27 Click **Greeting line**.

■ The Greeting Line dialog box appears.

■ These areas display the available formats for the greeting. You can click ▾ in an area to select a different format.

■ This area displays a preview of how the greeting will appear in the letter.

28 Click **OK** to add the greeting to the letter.

How do I delete a merge field I accidentally inserted?

To delete a merge field you accidentally inserted, drag the mouse I over the merge field until you highlight the field. Then press the Delete key.

When previewing the letters, can I exclude a person from the mail merge?

Yes. When the letter you do not want to send is displayed on your screen, click the **Exclude this recipient** button on the Mail Merge task pane. Word will not create a letter for the person when you complete the mail merge.

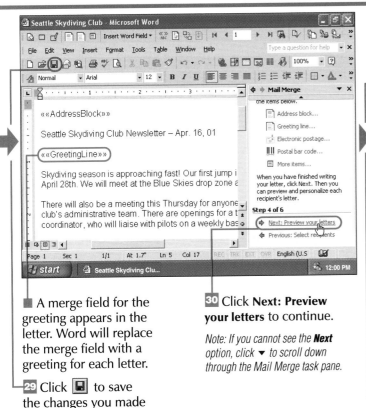

■ A merge field for the greeting appears in the letter. Word will replace the merge field with a greeting for each letter.

29 Click 💾 to save the changes you made to the letter.

30 Click **Next: Preview your letters** to continue.

*Note: If you cannot see the **Next** option, click ▼ to scroll down through the Mail Merge task pane.*

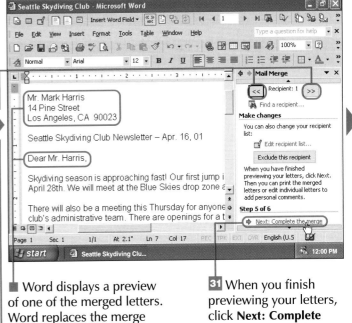

■ Word displays a preview of one of the merged letters. Word replaces the merge fields with the corresponding information for one person on your mailing list.

■ To preview another letter, click ◄◄ or ►► to display the previous or next letter.

31 When you finish previewing your letters, click **Next: Complete the merge** to continue.

CONTINUED

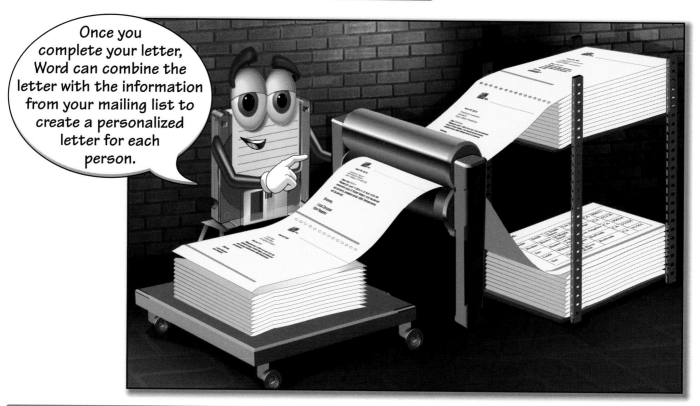

Once you complete your letter, Word can combine the letter with the information from your mailing list to create a personalized letter for each person.

CREATE LETTERS USING MAIL MERGE (CONTINUED)

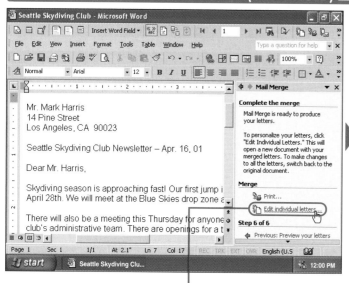

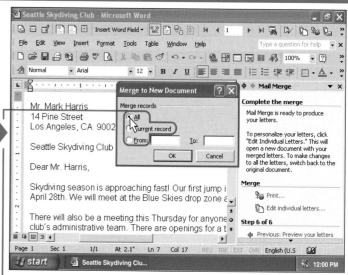

■ Word is ready to produce the letters.

32 Click **Edit individual letters** to combine the letter with the information from your mailing list.

■ The Merge to New Document dialog box appears.

33 Click an option to specify which people from your mailing list you want to create letters for (○ changes to ⊙).

All
All people on your mailing list.

Current record
Only the displayed person.

From
People on your mailing list that you specify.

Can I print the letters from the Mail Merge Wizard?

Yes. Printing letters from the Mail Merge Wizard is useful when you know the letters are ready to print and do not require further editing. To print your letters from the Mail Merge Wizard, select the **Print** option in step **32** below.

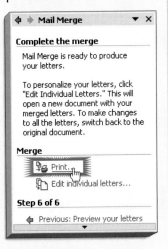

Should I save the document containing the personalized letters?

There is no need to save the document. You can easily perform another mail merge at any time to recreate the personalized letters.

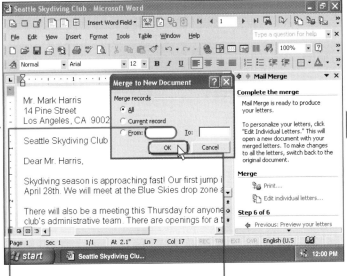

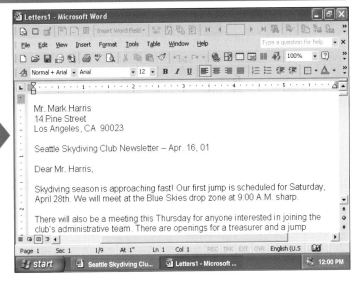

■ If you selected **From** in step **33**, click this area and type the number of the first person you want to create a letter for. Then press the **Tab** key and type the number of the last person you want to create a letter for.

34 Click **OK** to create the letters.

■ Word opens a new document and creates the personalized letters in the document.

■ You can edit and print the letters as you would edit and print any document. Editing a letter allows you to include additional information in the letter. To edit a document, see page 46. To print a document, see page 134.

CREATE LABELS USING MAIL MERGE

You can use
the Mail Merge feature
to print a personalized label
for each person on your
mailing list. This saves you
from having to type each
label individually.

You can use labels for addressing envelopes and packages.

The Mail Merge Wizard takes you step by step through the mail merge process.

CREATE LABELS USING MAIL MERGE

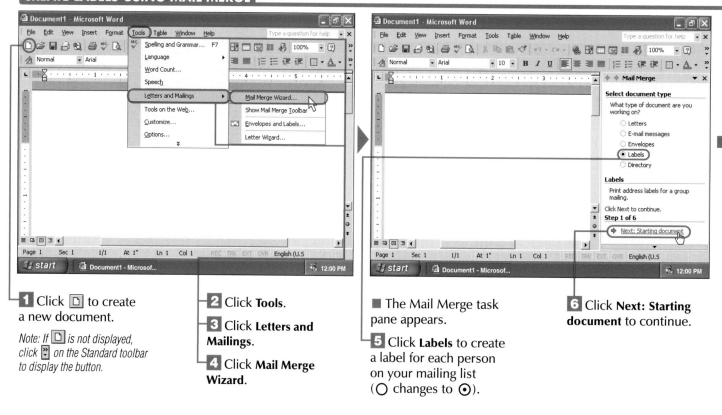

1 Click 🗋 to create a new document.

Note: If 🗋 is not displayed, click ❖ on the Standard toolbar to display the button.

2 Click **Tools**.

3 Click **Letters and Mailings**.

4 Click **Mail Merge Wizard**.

■ The Mail Merge task pane appears.

5 Click **Labels** to create a label for each person on your mailing list (○ changes to ⊙).

6 Click **Next: Starting document** to continue.

Can I use the Mail Merge Wizard to print envelopes?

Yes. You can use the Mail Merge Wizard to print a personalized envelope for each person on your mailing list. Perform steps **1** to **5** below, selecting **Envelopes** in step **5**. Then follow the instructions on your screen to set up the envelopes.

Can I create labels without using the Mail Merge Wizard?

Yes. If you want to create only a few labels, you can type the text you want to appear on each label yourself. For information on printing labels without using the Mail Merge Wizard, see page 138.

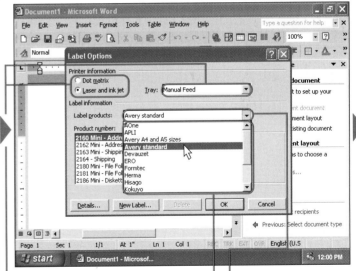

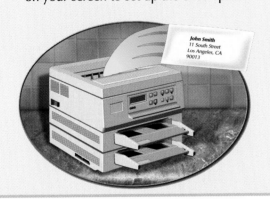

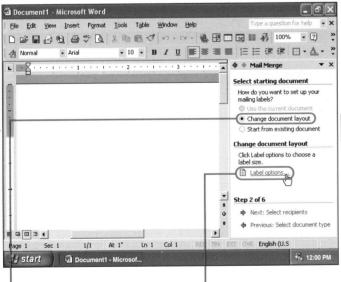

7 Click **Change document layout** to set up the current document for labels (○ changes to ⊙).

8 Click **Label options** to specify options for the labels.

■ The Label Options dialog box appears.

9 Click an option to specify the type of printer you will use to print the labels (○ changes to ⊙).

■ This area displays the printer tray that will contain the labels. You can click this area to specify a different tray.

10 Click this area to display a list of the available label products.

11 Click the label product you will use.

CONTINUED ▶

CREATE LABELS USING MAIL MERGE

After Word sets up a document for the labels, you must specify which mailing list stores the address information you want to appear on the labels.

CREATE LABELS USING MAIL MERGE (CONTINUED)

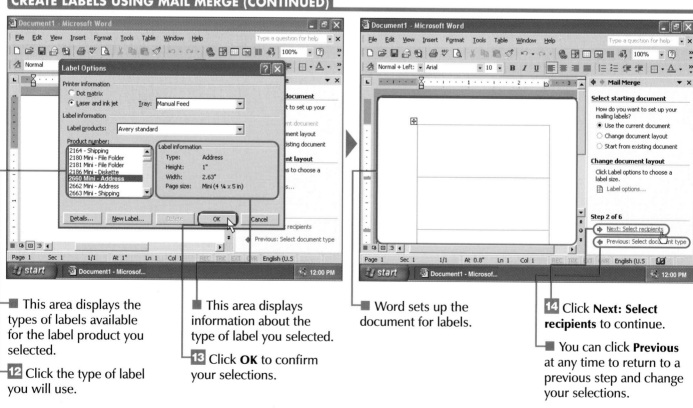

■ This area displays the types of labels available for the label product you selected.

12 Click the type of label you will use.

■ This area displays information about the type of label you selected.

13 Click **OK** to confirm your selections.

■ Word sets up the document for labels.

14 Click **Next: Select recipients** to continue.

■ You can click **Previous** at any time to return to a previous step and change your selections.

Which label product and type should I choose?

You can check your label packaging to determine which label product and type you should choose when printing labels.

Can I create a mailing list when I create labels?

If you have not created a mailing list that stores the address information you want to use, you can create a mailing list during the process of creating labels. After performing step 14 below, perform steps 11 to 18 starting on page 186 to create a mailing list for the labels. Then skip to step 19 on page 198 to continue with the mail merge.

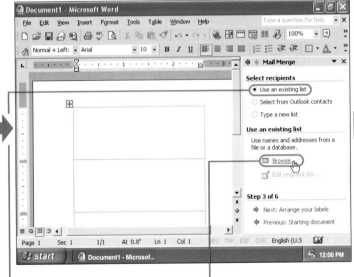

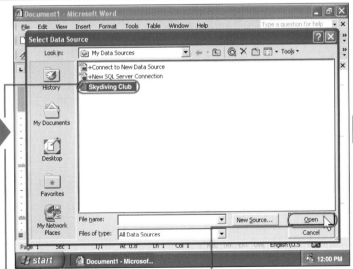

15 Click **Use an existing list** to use a mailing list you created in a previous mail merge (○ changes to ●).

Note: If you have not previously created a mailing list, see the top of this page.

16 Click **Browse** to select the mailing list you want to use.

■ The Select Data Source dialog box appears.

17 Click the file that stores the mailing list you want to use.

18 Click **Open** to open the file.

■ The Mail Merge Recipients dialog box appears.

CONTINUED

CREATE LABELS USING MAIL MERGE

Word displays the information for each person on your mailing list. You can select each person you want to create a label for.

CREATE LABELS USING MAIL MERGE (CONTINUED)

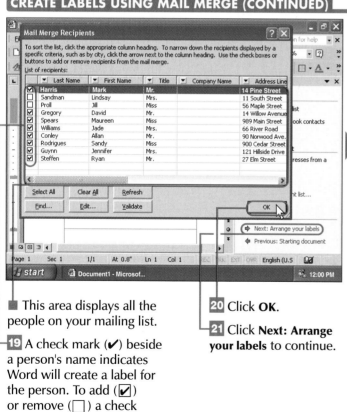

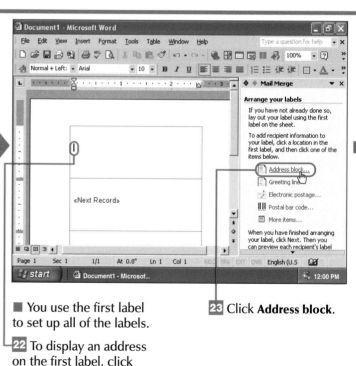

■ This area displays all the people on your mailing list.

19 A check mark (✔) beside a person's name indicates Word will create a label for the person. To add (☑) or remove (☐) a check mark, click the box beside a person's name.

20 Click **OK**.

21 Click **Next: Arrange your labels** to continue.

■ You use the first label to set up all of the labels.

22 To display an address on the first label, click the location on the label where you want to display the address.

23 Click **Address block**.

Can I sort my mailing list?

You can sort your mailing list when the Mail Merge Recipients dialog box is displayed. To sort your mailing list, click the heading of the column you want to use to sort the list. For example, if you want to sort the list alphabetically by last name, click the **Last Name** column heading.

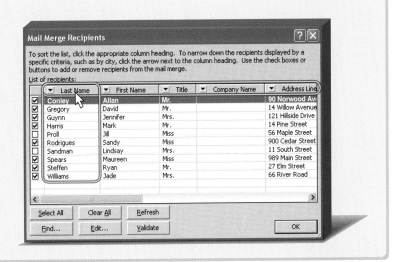

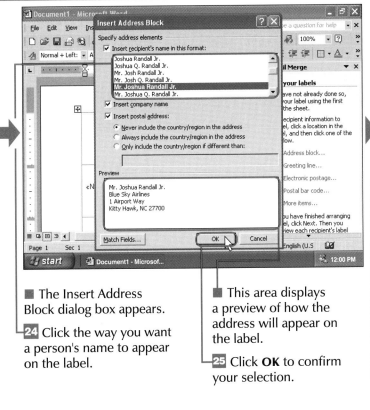

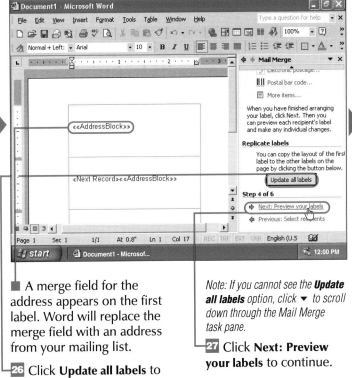

■ The Insert Address Block dialog box appears.

24 Click the way you want a person's name to appear on the label.

■ This area displays a preview of how the address will appear on the label.

25 Click **OK** to confirm your selection.

■ A merge field for the address appears on the first label. Word will replace the merge field with an address from your mailing list.

26 Click **Update all labels** to copy the layout of the first label to all the other labels.

*Note: If you cannot see the **Update all labels** option, click ▼ to scroll down through the Mail Merge task pane.*

27 Click **Next: Preview your labels** to continue.

CONTINUED

CREATE LABELS USING MAIL MERGE

> After you finish setting up your labels, Word can combine the labels with the information from your mailing list to create a personalized label for each person.

CREATE LABELS USING MAIL MERGE (CONTINUED)

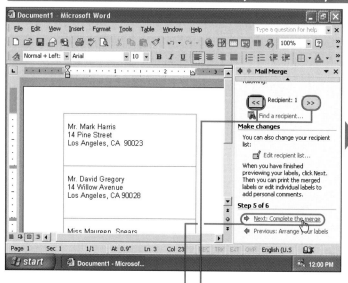

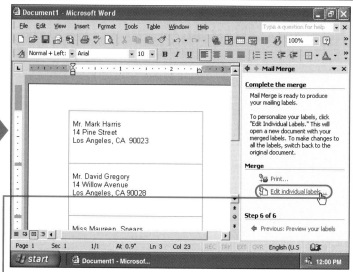

■ Word displays a preview of one page of the labels. Word replaces the merge fields with the corresponding information from your mailing list.

■ To preview other labels, click ⏴⏴ or ⏵⏵ to display the previous or next label at the top of the page.

28 When you finish previewing your labels, click **Next: Complete the merge** to continue.

■ Word is ready to produce the labels.

29 Click **Edit individual labels** to combine the labels with the information from your mailing list.

■ The Merge to New Document dialog box appears.

SIMPLIFY IT

Which people on my mailing list
can I create labels for?

All

Creates labels for all the
people on your mailing list.

Current record

Creates labels for only the people
shown on the current page.

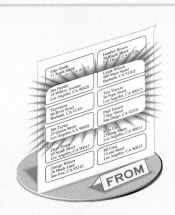

From

Creates labels for people on
your mailing list that you specify.

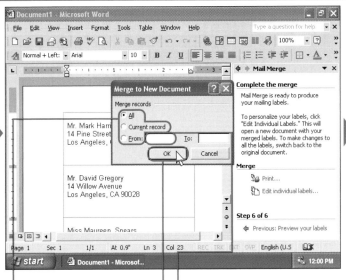

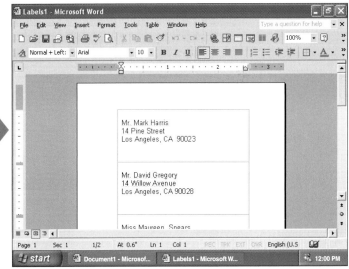

30 Click an option to
specify which people
on your mailing list you
want to create labels
for (○ changes to ⊙).

■ If you selected **From** in
step **30**, click this area and
type the number of the
first person you want to
create a label for. Then press
the Tab key and type the
number of the last person
you want to create a label for.

31 Click **OK** to create the
labels.

■ Word opens a new
document and creates
the personalized labels
in the document.

■ You can edit and print the
labels as you would edit and
print any document. Editing
a label allows you to include
additional information on the
label. To edit a document, see
page 46. To print a document,
see page 134.

201

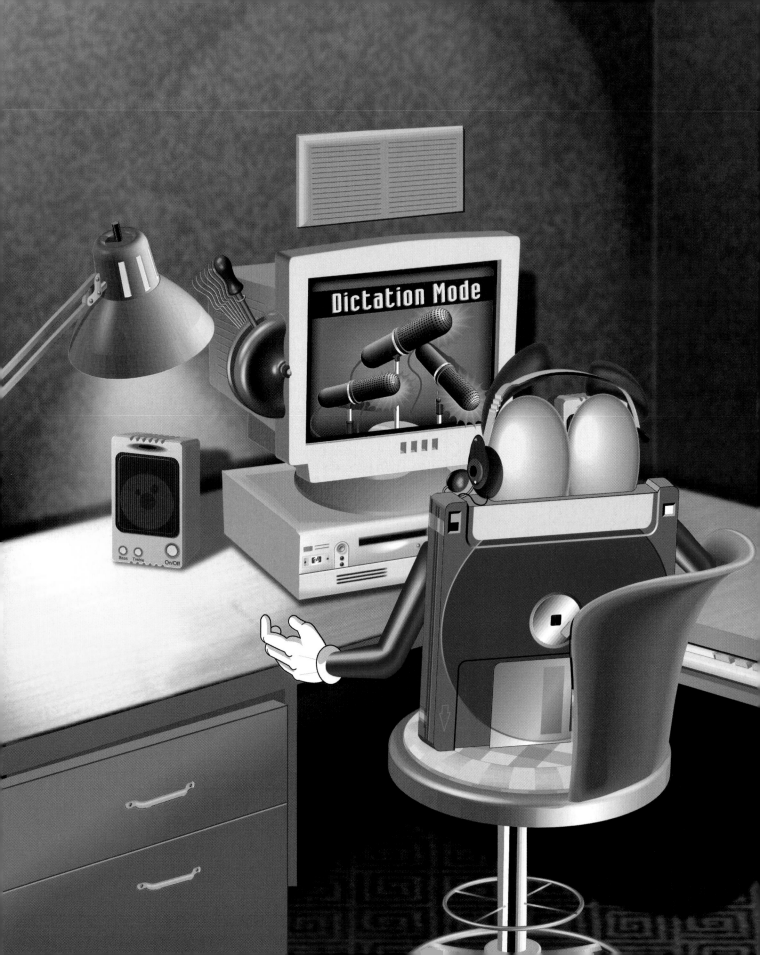

CHAPTER 11

USING SPEECH RECOGNITION

Would you like to use your voice to enter text into a document? Read this chapter to learn how to enter text and select commands using your voice.

SET UP SPEECH RECOGNITION

I am using Office Speech Recognition.

Speech recognition allows you to use your voice to enter text into a document and select commands from menus and toolbars. Before you can use speech recognition, you must set up the feature on your computer.

Before setting up speech recognition, make sure your microphone is connected to your computer.

It will take you approximately 15 minutes to set up speech recognition on your computer.

SET UP SPEECH RECOGNITION

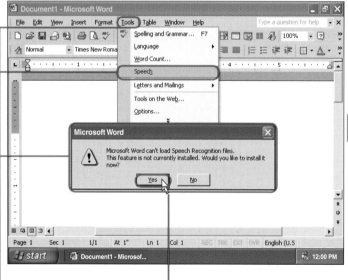

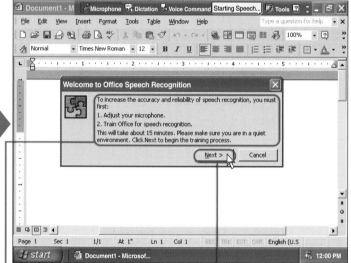

1 Click **Tools**.

2 Click **Speech**.

■ A message appears, stating that speech recognition is not currently installed.

3 Insert the CD-ROM disc you used to install Word into your computer's CD-ROM drive.

4 Click **Yes** to install speech recognition on your computer.

Note: A window may appear on your screen. Click ✕ in the top right corner of the window to close the window.

■ When the installation is complete, the Welcome to Office Speech Recognition dialog box appears.

■ This area describes the process of setting up speech recognition on your computer.

5 To begin setting up speech recognition, click **Next**.

Why does this dialog box appear when I try to set up speech recognition?

This dialog box appears if your computer does not meet the minimum hardware requirements needed to use speech recognition. You cannot set up speech recognition if your computer does not meet the minimum hardware requirements.

What type of microphone should I use with speech recognition?

You should use a headset microphone, since this type of microphone will remain in the correct position, even when you move your head. For best results, you should position the microphone approximately one inch from the side of your mouth so that you are not breathing directly into the microphone.

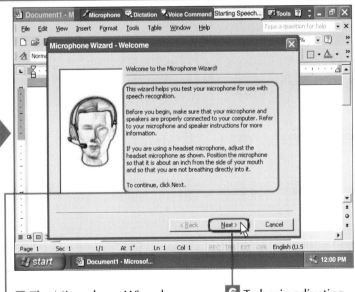

■ The Microphone Wizard appears. The wizard will help you adjust your microphone for use with speech recognition.

■ This area describes the wizard and provides instructions for positioning your microphone.

6 To begin adjusting your microphone, click **Next**.

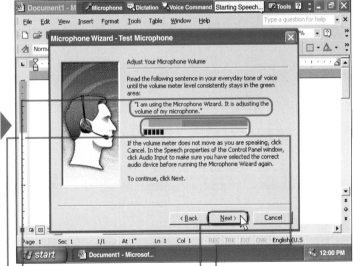

7 Read the text displayed in this area aloud to adjust the volume of your microphone.

■ As you read the text aloud, the volume meter in this area indicates the volume of your microphone.

8 Repeat step 7 until the volume level of your microphone consistently appears in the green area of the volume meter.

9 Click **Next** to continue.

CONTINUED

SET UP SPEECH RECOGNITION

You can train speech recognition to recognize how you speak. The Microsoft Speech Recognition Training Wizard takes you step by step through the process of training speech recognition.

You can listen to a sample sentence to hear how you should speak during the training.

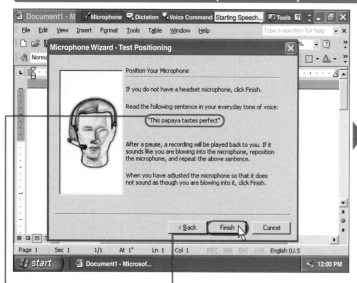

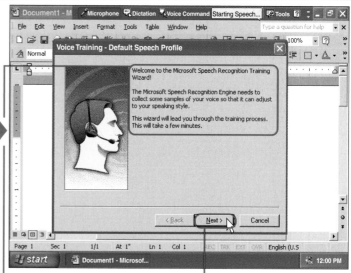

10 Read this text aloud to test the position of your microphone.

■ After a few moments, your voice will be played back to you. If it sounds like you are blowing into the microphone, adjust your microphone's position and then repeat step **10**.

11 When you finish positioning your microphone, click **Finish**.

■ The Microsoft Speech Recognition Training Wizard appears. This wizard will help you train speech recognition to recognize how you speak.

■ This area describes the wizard.

12 To begin training speech recognition to recognize how you speak, click **Next**.

Do I have to train speech recognition?

Yes. If you do not train speech recognition, the feature will not work properly. During the training, the Microsoft Speech Recognition Training Wizard gathers information about your voice. The speech recognition feature uses this information to recognize the words you say when entering text in a document or selecting commands.

How should I speak during the training process?

You should speak in your everyday tone of voice, pronouncing words clearly and not pausing between words. You should also speak at a consistent speed.

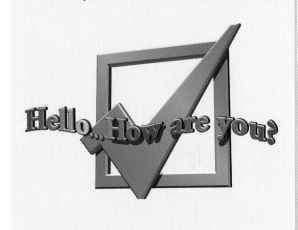

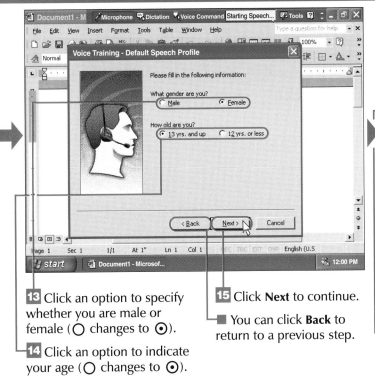

13 Click an option to specify whether you are male or female (○ changes to ⊙).

14 Click an option to indicate your age (○ changes to ⊙).

15 Click **Next** to continue.

■ You can click **Back** to return to a previous step.

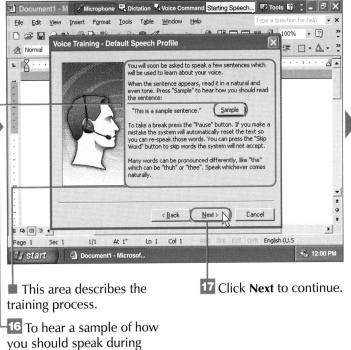

■ This area describes the training process.

16 To hear a sample of how you should speak during the training, click **Sample**.

17 Click **Next** to continue.

CONTINUED

The Microsoft Speech Recognition Training Wizard provides text you can read aloud to train speech recognition.

You should train speech recognition in a quiet area so that background noise does not interfere with the sound of your voice.

SET UP SPEECH RECOGNITION (CONTINUED)

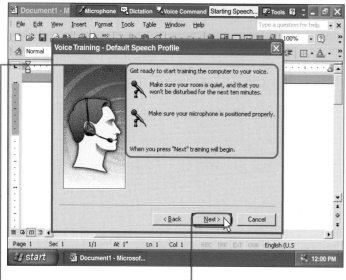

■ This area displays instructions about preparing for the training.

18 To begin the training, click **Next**.

■ The wizard will display a series of screens containing text for you to read aloud.

19 Read the text displayed in this area.

■ As you read aloud, the wizard highlights the words it recognizes.

■ If the wizard does not recognize a word, it stops highlighting text. If this happens, begin reading again, starting with the first word that is not highlighted.

I have repeated a word several times, but the wizard still does not recognize the word. What should I do?

If the wizard cannot recognize a word you say, you can click the **Skip Word** button to move on to the next word.

Can I perform more training?

The speech recognition feature provides additional training sessions you can perform to improve the accuracy of speech recognition.

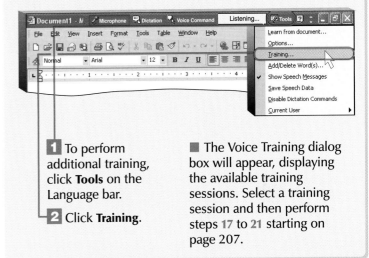

■ To perform additional training, click **Tools** on the Language bar.

② Click **Training**.

■ The Voice Training dialog box will appear, displaying the available training sessions. Select a training session and then perform steps **17** to **21** starting on page 207.

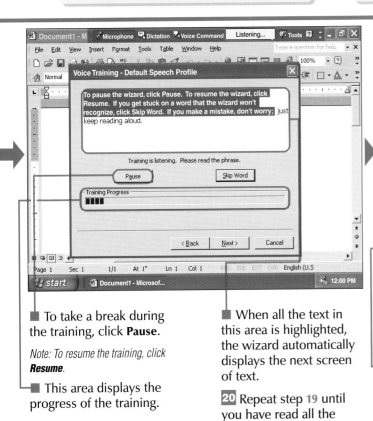

■ To take a break during the training, click **Pause**.

*Note: To resume the training, click **Resume**.*

■ This area displays the progress of the training.

■ When all the text in this area is highlighted, the wizard automatically displays the next screen of text.

20 Repeat step **19** until you have read all the training text.

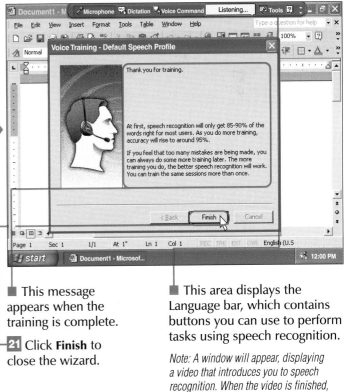

■ This message appears when the training is complete.

21 Click **Finish** to close the wizard.

■ This area displays the Language bar, which contains buttons you can use to perform tasks using speech recognition.

Note: A window will appear, displaying a video that introduces you to speech recognition. When the video is finished, click ✕ to close the window.

USING DICTATION MODE

Once you have set up speech recognition on your computer, you can use Dictation mode to enter text into a document using your voice.

Speech recognition is designed to be used along with your mouse and keyboard. You can use your voice to enter text into a document and then use your mouse and keyboard to edit the text you entered.

USING DICTATION MODE

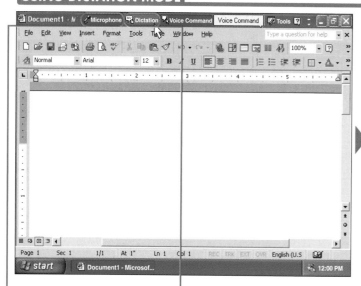

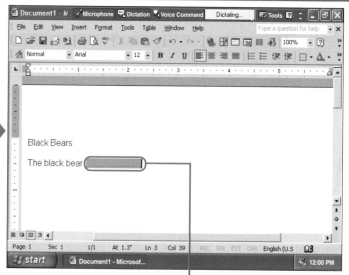

1 If your microphone is turned off, click **Microphone** on the Language bar to turn on the microphone.

Note: When your microphone is turned on, the Dictation and Voice Command buttons appear on the Language bar.

2 Click **Dictation** to turn on Dictation mode.

3 Speak into your microphone to enter text into the document.

Note: The text will appear where the insertion point flashes on your screen.

■ As you speak, a blue bar appears on the screen to indicate that the computer is processing your voice. You can continue to speak while the blue bar is displayed on the screen.

■ You should not use your mouse or keyboard while the blue bar is displayed on the screen.

What are some of the punctuation marks I can enter using my voice?

To enter:	Say:
.	"Period"
,	"Comma"
:	"Colon"
;	"Semicolon"
?	"Question mark"
!	"Exclamation point"
(	"Open parenthesis"
)	"Close parenthesis"
"	"Open quote"
"	"Close quote"
a new line	"New line"
a new paragraph	"New paragraph"

How should I speak when using speech recognition?

You should speak to your computer in your everyday tone of voice, pronouncing words clearly and not pausing between words. You should also speak at a consistent speed. If you speak too quickly or too slowly, the computer may not be able to recognize what you say.

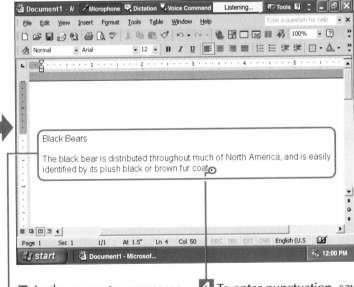

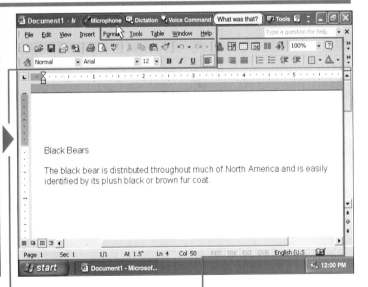

■ As the computer processes your voice, words appear on the screen.

4 To enter punctuation, say the name of the punctuation mark you want to enter.

Note: For a list of punctuation marks you can enter using your voice, see the top of this page.

■ As you enter text using your voice, this area may display a message to help you use Dictation mode. For example, the message "What was that?" indicates you should repeat your last words.

5 When you finish entering text using your voice, click **Microphone** to turn off your microphone.

■ You can now edit the text you entered using your voice as you would edit any text. To edit text, see page 46.

USING VOICE COMMAND MODE

You can use Voice Command mode to select commands from menus and toolbars using your voice.

You can also use Voice Command mode to select options in dialog boxes.

USING VOICE COMMAND MODE

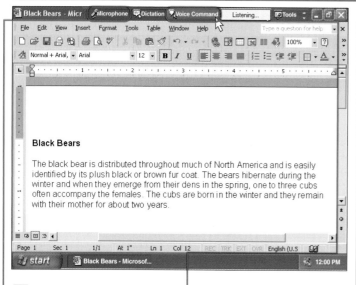

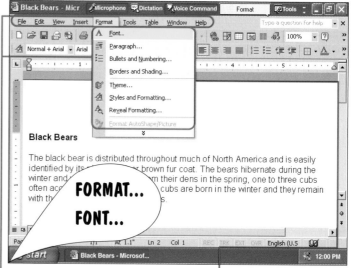

1 If your microphone is turned off, click **Microphone** on the Language bar to turn on the microphone.

Note: When your microphone is turned on, the Dictation and Voice Command buttons appear on the Language bar.

2 Click **Voice Command** to turn on Voice Command mode.

SELECT MENU COMMANDS

1 To select a command from a menu, say the name of the menu.

■ A short version of the menu appears, displaying the most commonly used commands.

Note: To expand the menu and display all the commands, say "expand."

2 To select a command from the menu, say the name of the command.

■ To close a menu without selecting a command, say "escape."

Can I use Voice Command mode to select an option in the task pane?

The task pane displays options that allow you to perform common tasks. To select an option in the task pane using your voice, say the full name of the option. For more information on the task pane, see page 16.

Can I use Voice Command mode to perform other tasks?

Yes. In addition to selecting commands, you can use Voice Command mode to perform the following tasks.

To:	Say:
Move up one line	"Up"
Move down one line	"Down"
Move left one character	"Left"
Move right one character	"Right"
Enter a tab	"Tab"
Enter a blank space	"Space"
Delete a character	"Backspace"

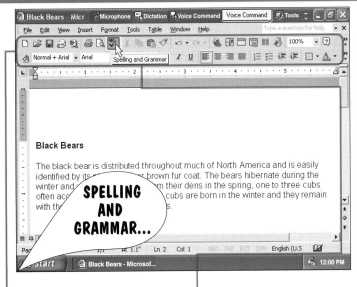

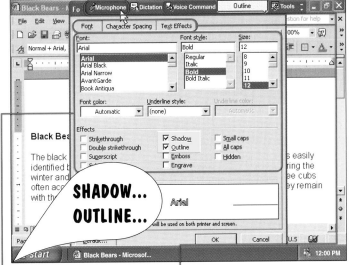

SELECT TOOLBAR COMMANDS

■1 To select a command from a toolbar, say the name of the toolbar button.

■ To determine the name of a toolbar button, position the mouse ▷ over the button. After a few seconds, the name of the button appears in a yellow box.

SELECT DIALOG BOX OPTIONS

■ A dialog box may appear when you select a menu or toolbar command.

■1 To select an option in a dialog box, say the name of the option.

■ If the dialog box contains tabs, you can say the name of a tab to display the tab.

■2 When you finish selecting commands using your voice, click **Microphone** to turn off your microphone.

Boston Cycling Club

Welcome to the Boston Cycling Club Network. We have been riding in Boston for 15 years and we are still going strong. To learn about the club, click one of the following links.

Boston Cycling Club Newsletter

List of Upcoming Events Organized by the Club

History of the Boston Cycling Club

How to Become a Member

Contact Information

CHAPTER 12

WORD AND THE INTERNET

Are you wondering how you can use Word to share information with other people on the Internet? In this chapter, you will learn how to e-mail a document, save a document as a Web page and more.

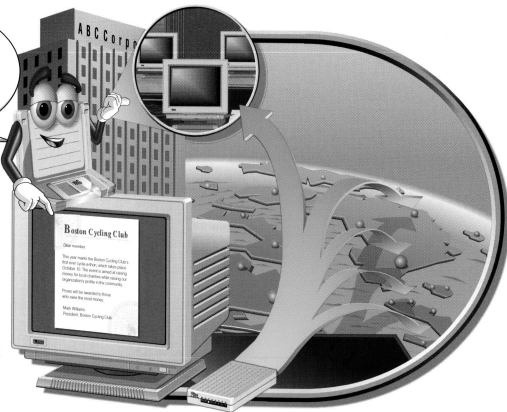

You can e-mail the document displayed on your screen to a friend, family member or colleague.

Before you can e-mail a document, an e-mail program, such as Microsoft Outlook, must be set up on your computer.

E-MAIL A DOCUMENT

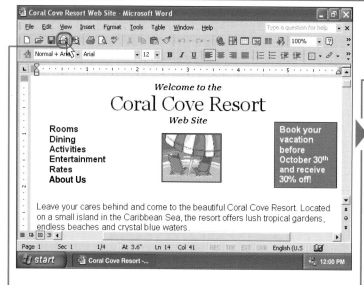

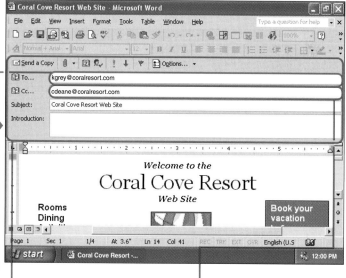

1 Click 🖳 to e-mail the displayed document.

Note: If 🖳 is not displayed, click ☒ on the Standard toolbar to display the button.

■ An area appears for you to address the message.

2 Click this area and type the e-mail address of the person you want to receive the message.

3 To send a copy of the message to another person, click this area and type their e-mail address.

*Note: To enter more than one e-mail address in step **2** or **3**, separate each e-mail address with a semicolon (;).*

How can I address an e-mail message?

To

Sends the message to the person you specify.

Carbon Copy (Cc)

Sends an exact copy of the message to a person who is not directly involved, but would be interested in the message.

Why would I include an introduction for the document I am e-mailing?

Including an introduction allows you to provide the recipient of the message with additional information about the document. For example, the recipient may require instructions or an explanation of the content of the document.

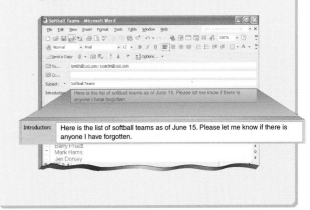

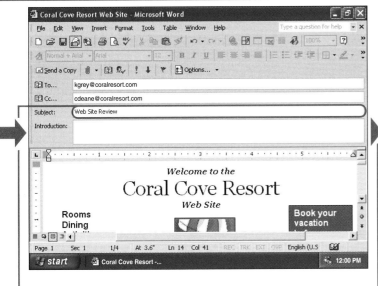

4 Click this area and type a subject for the message.

Note: If a subject already exists, you can drag the mouse I over the existing subject and then type a new subject.

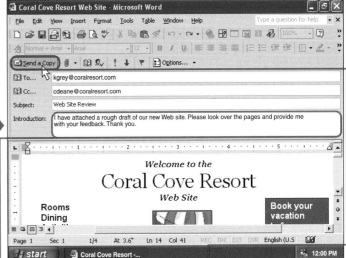

5 To include an introduction for the document you are e-mailing, click this area and type the introduction.

Note: You can include an introduction only if you are using the Microsoft Outlook e-mail program.

6 Click **Send a Copy** to send the message.

Note: If you are not currently connected to the Internet, a dialog box may appear, allowing you to connect.

217

CREATE A HYPERLINK

You can create a hyperlink to connect a word, phrase or graphic in your document to another document or Web page on your computer, network or the Internet.

CREATE A HYPERLINK

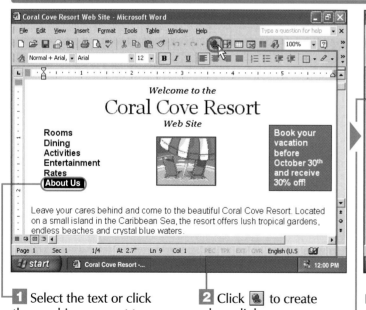

1 Select the text or click the graphic you want to link to another document or Web page. To select text, see page 10.

2 Click 📎 to create a hyperlink.

Note: If 📎 is not displayed, click ≫ on the Standard toolbar to display the button.

■ The Insert Hyperlink dialog box appears.

3 Click **Existing File or Web Page**.

■ This area shows the location of the displayed documents. You can click this area to change the location.

218

Can Word automatically create a hyperlink for me?

When you type the address of a Web page and then press the **Spacebar** or the `Enter` key, Word will automatically change the address to a hyperlink.

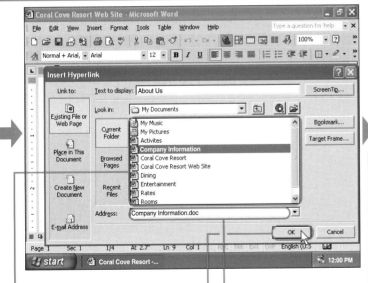

How can I remove a hyperlink?

To remove a hyperlink completely, select the text or click the graphic and then press the `Delete` key. To select text, see page 10.

To remove a hyperlink but keep the text or graphic, right-click the hyperlink and then select **Remove Hyperlink** from the menu that appears.

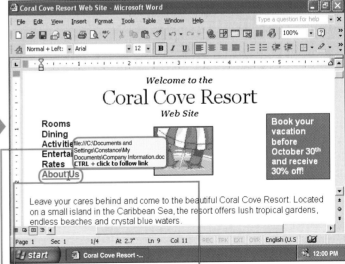

4 To link the text or graphic to a document on your computer or network, click the name of the document in this area.

■ To link the text or graphic to a page on the Web, click this area and then type the address of the Web page.

5 Click **OK** to create the hyperlink.

■ Word creates the hyperlink. Text hyperlinks appear underlined and in color.

■ When you position the mouse I over a hyperlink, a yellow box appears, indicating where the hyperlink will take you.

■ To display the document or Web page connected to the hyperlink, press and hold down the `Ctrl` key as you click the hyperlink.

SAVE A DOCUMENT AS A WEB PAGE

You can save a document as a Web page. This allows you to place the document on the Internet or your company's intranet.

An intranet is a small version of the Internet within a company or organization.

SAVE A DOCUMENT AS A WEB PAGE

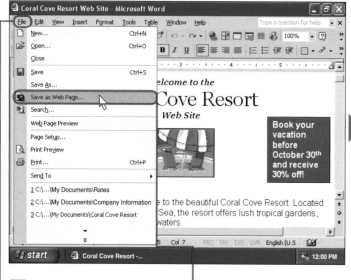

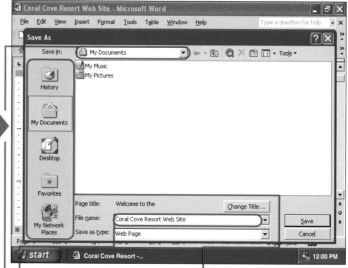

1 Open the document you want to save as a Web page. To open a document, see page 26.

2 Click **File**.

3 Click **Save as Web Page**.

■ The Save As dialog box appears.

4 Type a file name for the Web page.

■ This area shows the location where Word will store the Web page. You can click this area to change the location.

■ This area allows you to access commonly used locations. You can click a location to save the Web page in the location.

Note: For information on the commonly used locations, see the top of page 23.

What is the difference between the file name and the title of a Web page?

The file name is the name you use to store the Web page on your computer. The title is the text that will appear at the top of the Web browser window when a person views your Web page.

How do I make my Web page available for other people to view?

After you save a document as a Web page, you can transfer the page to a computer that stores Web pages, called a Web server. Once the Web page is stored on a Web server, the page will be available for other people to view. For information on transferring a Web page to a Web server, contact your network administrator or Internet service provider.

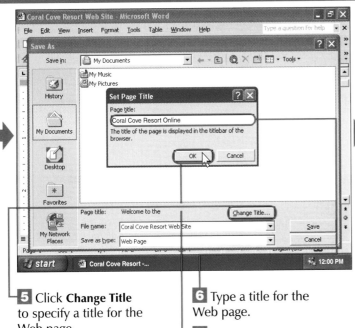

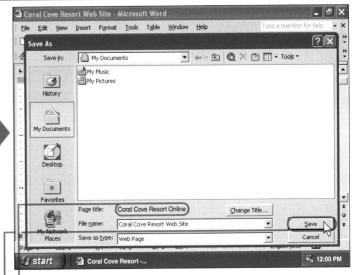

5 Click **Change Title** to specify a title for the Web page.

■ The Set Page Title dialog box appears.

Note: A default title may appear in the dialog box.

6 Type a title for the Web page.

7 Click **OK** to confirm the title.

■ This area displays the title you specified for the Web page.

8 Click **Save** to save the document as a Web page.

■ Word saves the document as a Web page and displays the document in the Web Layout view. This view displays the document as it will appear on the Web. For more information on the Web Layout view, see page 36.

INDEX